HEAVEN NEXT STOP

A Luftwaffe Fighter Pilot at War

HEAVEN NEXT STOP

A Luftwaffe Fighter Pilot at War

GUNTHER BLOEMERTZ

HOWELL PRESS

First published in 1953 by William Kimber & Co. Ltd

Published in the UK in 1996 by
Sutton Publishing Limited · Phoenix Mill
Thrupp · Stroud · Gloucestershire · GL5 2BU

Published in the United States in 1997 by
Howell Press Inc · 1147 River Road
Suite 2 · Charlottesville · VA 22901

Library of Congress Cataloging in Publication Data available

ISBN 1-57427-070-2

Printed in Great Britain by
Hartnolls Limited
Bodmin, Cornwall.

PUBLISHER'S NOTE

TO appreciate this book fully, one should have a very general knowledge of the command structure of the fighter-arm of the German Luftwaffe, so as to understand the significance of certain words which have necessarily been left in their original German, as there is no proper equivalent in English.

The smallest tactical formation to which reference is made is a *Rotte*, which consisted generally speaking of two to three aircraft, the leader of such a tactical unit being known as the *Rottenführer*. The smallest administrative Luftwaffe unit, a unit which was also employed tactically, was the *Schwarm*, of four to five aircraft. In flight, the leader of this would be known as *Schwarmführer*. A number of such *Schwärme*, say three to five, formed the *Staffel*, whose commanding officer is referred to in the book as *Staffelkapitän*, or sometimes just *Kapitän*, irrespective of his actual rank. He was usually a *Hauptmann* (captain) or a Major, was referred to colloquially as "Chief", and when leading his *Staffel* in the air as *Staffelführer*. Three *Staffel* customarily went to form the *Gruppe*, whose commanding officer was known as the *Kommandeur*, again irrespective of his actual rank in the Luftwaffe. Three *Gruppen* made up a *Geschwader*, the largest administrative unit with which we are concerned in this book. The commanding officer of a *Geschwader* was entitled *Kommodore*. A *Fähnrich* was a qualified pilot of officer-status but not yet "commissioned" in our

7

sense of the word. This rank is translated throughout as "cadet-pilot", or simply "cadet". German fighter-squadrons normally had a Welfare Officer, and in this instance he held the rank of captain, or *Hauptmann*.

Friend Hein is a German colloquialism for "Death".

Flugzeugführer means simply "pilot".

CONTENTS

ILLUSTRATIONS

11

CHAPTER I

WHAT was it father said long ago—"You want to be an airman? Now think, my boy. Downstairs there's a family like ours: father, mother and child, saying grace before supper—and you want to go and drop a bomb into all this peacefulness!"

"No," I replied, "no, father, I want to be a fighter pilot, one of the ones who shoots bombers down."

Then I was stretching both hands out of the window of the railway carriage, with mother quietly crying and father saying in a low voice, "Come back safely, my . . ." The first flight over the fields and the wide forest, above the red tiled roofs of the town . . . the heavy suitcases when I arrived at the front. Oh—they *were* heavy! I had put them down and entered the dusty, dry barracks. That was in Abbeville . . . Abbeville—the front.

The spare man in the plain linen flying-suit standing before me was the Kommandeur of the Abbeville Boys. A bright yellow life jacket hung loosely across his shoulder and chest, and a black, white and red ribbon stood out from under his collar.

"How old?"

"Nineteen, Herr Major."

His lower lip came forward and he stared at me for a moment. "Have you any request to make?"

It sounded like an execution. But I did actually have a request—to get near two of my friends. Werner and Ulrich were a reminder of home. . . .

The sun-warmed air was shimmering above the long concrete runways and wide stretches of grass. I had to walk on for quite half an hour with my heavy cases to the other side of the airfield. Close above the horizon, far beyond the shimmering layer, something sparkled for a second. A dozen fine streaks lay mutely across the sky: twelve fighters were either flying away from me or would be over my head in a few seconds. The streaks grew larger. Soon cockpits, wings and armament could be made out—the aircraft were already flying so low over the grass that in the hot eddying air they seemed to fuse with the ground, and still I could hear no engine noise. I saw the heads behind the goggles, the blunt noses of the motors hurtling towards me. A thin singing hum grew momentarily louder, then they were roaring over my head in lightning and thunder—and away.

I turned my head. The twelve trails with their dots in front were once again high in the sky. So those were they: the Tommies called them the "Abbeville Boys," and feared and respected them.

"Line-shooters!" I said to myself.

The line-shooters returned. Banking steeply, they circled the airfield and then swept in to land, whistling and bellowing, sharp explosions punctuating the flat accompaniment of idly-turning propellers. For a fraction of a second they displayed their flat, silver-blue bellies, drew down ever more closely towards their shadows on the grass, and alighted carefully with legs spread wide. Perhaps that's my squadron, I thought, perhaps Werner and Ulrich are with them. Or had they already been killed? I hauled my suitcases on a bit further, spurred by the joyful anticipation of seeing two old friends again.

At that very moment, from the squadron dispersal area, a "bird" rose in a leisurely, awkward fashion into the air. Its engine roaring, it vibrated slowly along towards me, splaying out its thin stork-like legs as though about to land again any moment. In fact the 'Storch' landed scarcely thirty paces away on the greensward. The pilot jumped out, clowning in dumb show.

"Hallo, old boy! What a sight for my poor old eyes. You, too, taking your bones to market?"

Ulrich was standing before me: Ulrich, the dark-eyed, spare-framed reservist with the long, almost black hair—Ulrich, my pal of recruit days, who had worn his service nightshirt with such lazy distinction and had climbed every night into the topmost bunk of the row.

"Ulrich, old fellow, how did you know I was here?" I mumbled.

"Slow as ever in the uptake! How did I know you were here? Caught sight of you during the approach, recognised your old moon face quite plainly. Hawk's eyes, old boy—hawk's eyes! Cigarette?"

Ulrich's lapels smelt as they always had done of *Soir de Paris*.

"Incidentally, you look a regular porter," he went on unkindly. "There wasn't a car handy at the squadron but a Storch is just as good. Simple, isn't it? Coming?"

We went laughing to the aircraft. Ulrich's walk was as it used to be, leaning forward so you expected him to fall on his nose any moment. Around his mouth and at the corners of the eyes there had appeared finely drawn wrinkles.

"Yes, the Abbeville Boys have had a good deal of scrapping," he grinned. "And this evening we're going to drown it all."

"Where's Werner?" I asked, hesitating.

"Baled out an hour ago over St. Omer. Got a bit above himself. The little Spitfires gave him a bellyful.

15

Poor chap rang up just now. He's flying back with a replacement in the morning. Chuck your cigarette away!"

We climbed in to the cockpit of the Storch, and the shortest air journey of my career began. A few seconds later we climbed out between two dispersal hangars.

"The one in front is the Kapitän," Ulrich muttered under his breath. The Kapitän might well have been a cadet, for his fresh, brown face made him look just like an eighteen-year-old. The pilots were lying back in their easy chairs between the aircraft and waiting for the next sortie. The Kapitän led me round from one to the other, and Ulrich drew me finally to a chair next to his own.

The pair to my right were called Vogel and Meyer II, a strange couple who seemed only to exist for each other.

"The best of the whole squadron," whispered Ulrich, indicating them with his eyes.

The pilots' attention was jerked to the loudspeaker. Ulrich listened tautly with his lips pressed together. Only a hum could be heard at first—the current as it was switched on—and then came the announcement.

"*Achtung, achtung! Enemy aircraft forming up in strength over London, probably four-engined bombers.*"

Ulrich swallowed a curse. "Off we go again."

Drawing nervously at his cigarette he turned abruptly away, making for his machine. The other pilots were already clambering into their cockpits.

"*Immediate readiness!*" came through the loudspeaker, and the latecomers sprang into their aircraft. I stood on the wing beside Ulrich, who was crouched in the narrow cockpit, fastening his harness.

"Do your stuff!"

Laughing, he punched me in the chest.

"Can do," he nodded, and then, softly and nervously, "can do—can do. . . ."

His fists were clenched and I could see he had become suddenly serious. His eyes, lost in an unearthly distance, reflected something strange and rare, not fear—but perhaps a certain Figure with a scythe coming towards him across the wide field. Since I had got to know Ulrich it was this curious expression in the eyes which had led me to the fancy that he might be a visitor from another planet wishing to study affairs on earth, moving among human beings to experience their habits, joys and sorrows, so he, too, could love, fight and die like any of them.

"*Achtung! achtung! Squadron take off at once! Enemy formation airborne over Thames Estuary. Course Flushing.*"

The two-thousand-h.p. engines sprang into deafening life, their slip-stream forcing me backwards, as if eighty thousand horses were thundering all around. Forty small, compact single-seaters roared across the airfield, rose laboriously from the ground and drove with gathering speed towards the enemy.

That very day one of the pilots in our squadron had won his twenty-fifth victory in the air. In the evening a crowd of fellows came into our mess to celebrate in the company of their successful comrade. The Kommandeur with his staff, the Kapitäne of the neighbouring units and the pilots of our own squadron were all there. The men of the morning had changed very much in appearance, for instead of oily flying-suits they were wearing smart white or dark-blue uniforms, white shirts and—in accordance with a special squadron custom—loosely fitting white socks. Even in the Palace of Versailles you would not have found greater correctness in social conduct than here; but in spite of this, the conversation was pretty easy.

The Welfare Officer of our squadron was there too, a

reserve major who always wore uniforms of English cut. Known as "Papi," he could easily have been the father of any one of us. He got now to telling a story about the evening a strange guest had been entertained in a small chateau not far from St. Omer: a legendary Englishman who had already lost both his legs and who had now been shot down in combat. The brave Englishman had landed safely, but his artificial limbs had been smashed. So there was the captured enemy airman, the renowned Wing-Commander Bader from the other side, sitting in the middle of a group of German pilots—the Fighter General himself had invited him to an evening party.

The two of them, both experts at their craft, had sat in deep armchairs by the fireplace, their gaze fixed on the crackling embers. The atmosphere was rather oppressive, everyone appreciating the feelings of their guest, the airmen's immobile expressions flung into relief by the light of the flaming logs. No one spoke a word. Every now and again they sipped their drinks quietly and with reserve, never forgetting the little formalities which went with it. Germans are incapable of behaving in any other way—they honoured their guest as the man who had forgotten both his legs were missing to go out and fight for his country.

The strangeness of the occasion and reflections about their shot-down opponent led every man's thoughts the same way, suddenly to anathematize the war and that fate which throws a man into one particular society at his birth, and makes it his duty to conform to it. Why hadn't each of them been born in England? That would have given England one more pilot. Why was the Englishman sitting by the fireplace not a German? He might perhaps have been a kommodore of our own. Hadn't we often enough in peacetime sat down at table with those whom to-day it seemed our highest duty to kill? It was suddenly impossible to understand how men of the same sort, with the same feelings, desires, and needs could come to mangle one another to death.

The Englishman might well have been thinking somewhat similar thoughts, but he too had found himself unable to solve this problem and so perhaps had let it rest. At that, as he looked up, they raised their glasses to him. And subsequently there slowly developed between him and the German General an intimate discussion about fights experienced in common, told after the usual manner of fighter pilots—the sort of conversation only good friends can have.

That same evening the guest had asked if his reserve legs could be sent across from England, and a few hours afterwards a British radio operator was holding the message in his hands—the Germans had offered an escort at a pre-arranged time, at a specified point where the legs could be dropped by parachute. But over there they didn't seem to trust "the Jerries" very much, for next day the Germans received a message to the effect that the legs had been dropped at a different time and in another area.

Our close attention had rewarded the Major for his narrative. I had quite recently heard more about the remarkable R.A.F. officer who continuously encouraged his companions in the prisoner-of-war camps to escape. He had finally got away himself, and it was even suggested our General had given him encouragement in doing so: at any rate the former had sworn heartily when he heard the British party had been re-captured.

As the last words of the narrator died away a disconcerted silence settled over the company. Few of my fellow pilots had known that memorable fireside circle at the Chateau of St. Omer: the others were no longer living. It was not surprising we were silent.

The Kommandeur rose to his feet.

"*Kameraden!* The Abbeville Boys come, do their duty and go. They follow the example of their fallen friends with all that they have in them. These friends have bequeathed to us their knightly spirit. May every one of us carry this spirit in him, and hand it on even when the enemy wins a victory. To the health of all true knights!"

Subdued strains of jazz could be heard from the next room. I thought to myself—in every age there'll always be knights.

CHAPTER II

LATE that evening, with glasses of brandy in our hands, Ulrich and I received orders to take off at first light from a small airfield north of Abbeville. This field lay at the edge of the Forest of Crécy, and was one of those which the English had used during the First World War. From it we were to intercept two Spitfires which used to fly over from Biggin Hill each morning at the same time and patrol along the coast. A reconnaissance at daylight from the English point of view was a small risk, comparable to that which defence against such early risers presented to us. But the Tommies didn't believe we ever sat ready in our aircraft at this hour, and we counted on this. For this reason both we and the English used to let a learner go out on these operations, a "guinea-pig" so to speak, this being the quickest way of giving him his baptism of fire.

And now I was the guinea-pig. It was striking six when I put my right leg out of bed. In an hour's time someone would be shooting at me and I would perhaps be training my guns for the first time on a human being.

I took things as they came, as millions had done before me, trying to banish all such thoughts from my mind. I looked at my "new" aircraft: perhaps I should soon be lying in the ground in company with it. But really it was so old one could almost attribute to it a consciousness and experience of its own; some people even maintained it could fly without a pilot and shoot down an enemy aircraft of its own accord. I put on my dressing-gown.

That moment there came the order: *"Tommies close off the mouth of the Somme. Take off at once!"*

The Englishmen would certainly not have spent last night drinking brandy! I ran to my machine. Ulrich, too, with puffy eyes and in pyjamas was hurrying to his aircraft. As the engine revved up someone threw a life-jacket round me and someone else fastened my parachute harness and belt.

Full throttle! As I left the ground and swept low over the tree tops of the Forest of Crécy beside Ulrich, I put on my helmet and goggles with my left hand, adjusted the R/T pads around my neck, retracted the under-carriage, raised the flaps, set the trimmer and made the innumerable small manual adjustments which were required.

We were already over the sea, with a visibility of barely a thousand metres. Then, through the grey, damp morning mist, the two Spitfires were all at once rushing towards us. To wrench the stick round, sight, turn, aim and fire was a matter of seconds in which body and brain acted with automatic precision—a mechanical reaction for which I had prepared myself for two years, against a target which I now hit quite without conscious volition or regard to the consequences. The enemy crumpled under my fire. Victory! A transport of happiness and pride possessed me, from which it took me a moment to recover. Finally I turned my aircraft and looked round with anxious eyes for Ulrich. Far astern, guns were sparkling in the clear sky over the mainland: the adversaries pursuing one another in a series of steep, tight turns. Before I could help, a small white mushroom unfolded, and slowly sank towards the earth. Ulrich's aircraft spun into a wood, and the Tommy flew on his way.

I circled low over my friend, whose pyjamas were flapping in the breeze. Ulrich waved to me, seemingly unhurt. He had scarcely landed in a small meadow when from all directions gallant infantrymen with rifles at the ready came hurrying to take him prisoner. They had obviously mistaken him for the defeated enemy and me for the victorious German. For the first time since the fight I actually began to laugh—Ulrich, the "captured Tommy" was standing down there in his pyjamas with his hands above his head!

I had too much to attend to in my machine to watch this spectacle for long, but I saw them taking Ulrich away, and I had already flown a good part of the journey home when I looked round again. To my horror I saw another aircraft on my quarter, apparently almost within touching distance. Just as well it wasn't a Tommy. The unknown pilot put his hand to his helmet, and I returned his salute. The other was smiling all over his face.

"Good morning, old man," came through on my earphones. I looked again, more closely.

"Werner, hallo Werner!"

I had to look ahead again, but now I understood. Werner had baled out yesterday near St. Omer and was now flying a new machine back to Abbeville. I looked across at him again—he was staring before him and spoke without turning his head.

"Are you landing at Abbeville?"

"Can't very well. Look at this!" I lifted the skirt of my dressing-gown to the window of the cockpit. It was a little while before Werner understood.

"Good show," he laughed. I didn't know whether he meant my dressing-gown, Ulrich's pyjamas or this strange reunion. And when, a few minutes later, I dropped away over Crécy and we waved to each other again it was as

23

though a few days only had passed, instead of five long years, since we had last seen one another.

That welcome night brought to an end what had been a difficult day. I lay awake and thought of the daylight hours just passed. They had been commonplace for many, decisive for some. Today, as for many years past, death and mourning, victory and ecstasy had been arbitrarily apportioned among us. Friend and foe alike had been under the same illusion as they said their prayers, of supplication or gratitude, hurriedly, humbly or proudly, each one wishing only to love the good and to hate evil. And we too belonged to that company.

From time to time we openly recognised the meaning-lessness of this existence. More often we simply sensed it. But, at moments like these, what could our disgust alone do against the links of this fateful chain made up of our own bodies and souls, dragging us all along? Good motives there were—here as well as "over there"—our own country, our own wives and children at home must be protected as stoutly as those on the other side. We young men were incapable of comprehending the mean-ing of it all. Fate plunged onwards down its ordained path, and however we might try to protect ourselves it struck us exactly as it pleased. I couldn't block its way; and you—you who had wanted to kill me early in the morning—you couldn't do so either. Tommy, if you still live, are you perhaps drinking at this moment in some bar in the West End? Or perhaps you're in some quiet corner, grieving over one of your own friends or squadron mates who died in the early morning; perhaps you're writing at this moment to his parents or his fiancée, who, still cheerful, have as yet no idea what has happened? Tommy, I know you would do that, just as I should.

How joyfully I grasped my comrades' hands! I jumped beaming from the cockpit, while a soul went up from the still warm body of a man I had killed. How proud I had still been in the time before the bell tolled for him whom I had shot.

The day passed in jollity, dancing and girls' laughter. I wanted to forget the morning, to wipe the vision of blood and shining roundels from before my eyes. Now the silent night lay over all. I was very tired, but I couldn't sleep. Agonising thoughts still passed through my head. Did every soldier experience this feeling when he had killed a man for the first time?

I listened to Ulrich's quiet breathing. Perhaps he would laugh if I asked him about it.

"You could have saved yourself the last burst!" he had said smilingly, not ironically or frivolously, and certainly not sadly. I could see it still, the Tommy in his Spitfire hovering in the air close in front of me. I have no idea whether I have hit him. But I fire—for whole seconds in my excitement. Then we go into turns, the tightest possible turns. It seems any moment I must go into a spin. The rough sea spray is scarcely a hundred metres below me, and we are far out from the shore. I am still lying not quite right astern of the enemy, and the correct deflection for hitting him has not yet been reached. Nerves are stretched to the uttermost. My quarry hauls his machine all of a sudden right round in front of me, so that heavy vapour-trails appear in the sky. I react instantaneously and take a chance between crashing the aircraft and getting the final ounce out of it. Heaving the stick towards me with both hands, for the fraction of a second I achieve the correct firing-angle. My index-finger shifts by a millimetre on the triggers of my guns, and the burst flashes into the enemy's fuselage.

25

He plunges almost vertically, but regains control just above the surface with desperate strength, and climbs steeply—mortally hit. I see him struggling to get out—he wants to jump. He's like a hunted quarry during any such chase and I feel with him—pray feverishly for him.

There she goes! The damaged aircraft's climbing vertically in front of me in its last convulsion, the great roundels on the wings standing out bright and hostile—filling me only with horror. In the seconds which decide a man's life my finger again crooks automatically one millimetre—and the burst streaks redly out!—I shudder. It shouldn't have happened, it wasn't necessary. But I can't bring those deadly jewels back; it's done now.

"Jump! man, jump!" I shout aloud in despair. Instead I see him bathed in the red of his own blood; his body strains half over the side to hang there, mutilated. Then the waves close over him. . . .

Perhaps it was only the trembling of my finger that brought death to that man? I didn't know. But again it came to me—how fate goes its own way and strikes us down as it pleases. I couldn't stop it, and nor could you—whoever you may have been.

I turned over on my pillow and reached for the reading-lamp and the cigarettes. For a long while I gazed meditatively at the pictures of my parents. Perhaps to-morrow they would be weeping for me.

"Still awake?" Ulrich asked softly, although he knew well I wasn't sleeping. He too was staring at the ceiling. "What are you thinking about?"

"What am I thinking about. . . ." I repeated, rather at a loss. It was a difficult question; as a soldier I had had to forget how to talk from the heart. But it was easier to talk lying there gazing upwards—you can speak so much more easily and naturally to the ceiling.

"What am I thinking about, Ulrich? The Tommy of this morning," I confessed. "It simply wasn't necessary. Why didn't the man jump before he did?"

"You must forget it," Ulrich replied. "One gets used to anything, including shooting people down . . . but even so, war's a pretty bloody business." We were silent. "But, you know," he began again after a pause, "it's a great deal bloodier for someone like me who does it all without any real conviction."

Nothing more was said. I don't know how long we lay there with our eyes open, and the light was still burning when the dawn woke us.

CHAPTER III

THE next morning we ran our wheels for the last time on to the field at the edge of the Forest of Crécy. Our job was done. The mechanics waved, and we flew off back to Abbeville, leaving the dewy grass of the long field behind us. Once more, as the slipstream from the propellers drew its wake through the treetops, the forest's inhabitants, great and small, hurried fearfully away, many a bird's heart beating wildly as the seven-league boots of the two giants raced overhead. Then quiet returned once more to the forest.

A few minutes later we landed on the smooth surface of our home airfield. When I jumped from my machine Werner was standing before me. I was disappointed. A stranger, I thought—he's just like a stranger. Five years had changed both of us, our paths had lain too far apart. I had gone from my parents' home and the schoolroom to the war, while Werner had come from a national-political educational establishment. His blond hair was carefully parted, his blue eyes held a more serious expression than of old, and he had grown into a giant. Only time would show whether he had changed in other ways.

We lay stretched out in our easy-chairs under the bright sky and waited for the approach of enemy aircraft, playing chess and skat and talking interminably on every conceivable subject, to kill time, to banish if we could the torture of waiting. Ulrich had moved to one side and was writing something, allowing no one to look over his shoulder. Werner sat next to me, and on the other side lay Vogel and Meyer II, together as usual.

"Are that couple quite normal?" I asked softly.

"Just as you please," Werner answered. "Except for their beds and their toothbrushes they have nothing they don't own in common. They've one camera, one car, one lighter—they read the same books, tell the same stories, hold the same rank, always fly together, register an identical number of victories and know no women. Each has several times saved the life of the other, and I am sure that if one of them should be killed, the other wouldn't live a day longer. Incidentally, they're the best of fellows, and superb pilots."

No one knew how and since when they had become so friendly. One had heard about Meyer II in the flying schools, for Meyer II was something of a celebrity in the traditions of the Luftwaffe, his story running something like this:

He had worked for years as a fitter, but his dearest wish had been to become a pilot himself, and this gave him no rest. It seemed hopeless for him ever to attain his object through regular channels, so he had begun to practise in secret on the controls of aircraft lying out at dispersal, accustoming himself to those necessary for taking off, flying and landing. For a full year he must have studied these innumerable buttons, knobs and handles, until finally he could work them in his sleep—in his everlasting dreams of flying. So at last the time had come when Meyer II felt himself ready. He took off, and circled cautiously above the airfield where his friends, watching his spirited efforts, tensely awaited the inevitable crash—they had heard of such attempts, but never before had one of these lunatics got away with his life. And Meyer II, furthermore, had taken it into his head to fly without a parachute.

29

His feet cramped on the rudder bar, the sweat of fear ran from every pore and his moist grip slipped on stick and throttle lever. Down below he could see his comrades grouped like tiny dots, and suddenly close to him he saw another aircraft, its pilot was signalling him to jump. Meyer II got such a fright that the rudder pedals almost slipped from his feet. Then he looked hastily ahead once more.

"Steady," said Meyer II to himself. "I, Obergefreiter Meyer II," he called out aloud, "I *will* keep steady! S-T-E-A-D-Y!" he roared, until the tears almost came to his eyes. But the little monologue had calmed him down and resolving now to complete the most difficult part of the whole affair, he drew the throttle lever slowly back, ready for landing. The aircraft dipped gently and sank towards the ground. Meyer II turned carefully to the left and circled the airfield in a succession of flat curves. Then the ground started to rush beneath him faster than ever. Throwing a glance at the air speed indicator and another at the position of his machine as the earth shot up to meet him, Meyer II knew full well that in the course of the next few seconds Death would have his opportunity—he was at the last few feet above the grass—just about the depth of a grave. Immediately in front of the aircraft's shadow a hare doubled on its tracks.

Meyer II cut his throttle. Everything went quiet all around him, and then he did the cleverest thing of his life. He drew the stick quite gently back towards him. The machine dropped heavily onto the ground, rocked, turned a full circle as though waltzing, and came to rest the wrong way round as in the finale of a harlequinade.

Meyer II was taken away to "Father Philip," the detention quarters for delinquents, to cool his heels with bread and water for six long weeks, with the choice of reading either the Bible or *Mein Kampf*. Only when he had endured all this was he finally sent to the kingdom of his dreams—the flying school. Now he was considered to be one of the most outstanding pilots in the whole squadron.

Werner burst into laughter beside me. The pilots had jumped from their chairs and hurriedly turned their backs on a passing tom-cat, so that their gaze should not meet that of this omen of bad luck. When the cat had passed the line of chairs, there arose a heated discussion about the sense or otherwise of superstition, every shade of belief coming trotting out. Ulrich belonged to the least serious category. He disliked number thirteen and swore he would never fly on a Friday if it happened to be the thirteenth of the month, as he would certainly be killed if he did so. I remembered one evening when he and I had been looking for a bed for the night. In the end we found a hotel where only room No. 13 was vacant. Late as it was, Ulrich had used a scrap of paper to change the number to 12A.

The oldest of our fellow-pilots was a far greater sufferer from such imaginings. He had already flown himself out and his nerves were in shreds. Whenever things went well he would knock three times with the joint of his right middle finger against wood. In the course of time this had got so bad that scarcely a minute went by but that he would be seen at his three-fold "lucky" tappings. I could almost see myself getting to the same pitch. Any thought which occurred to him containing anything the least bit unpleasant made him feel it must somehow be transmuted into good—a longing which manifested itself a hundred times a day. He had made himself believe the fulfilment of this wish depended on tapping, hence he always carried with him, together with the compass, Very lights, distress signals and coloured bag which he wore strapped to his leg, a piece of wood.

Something of the sort was discernible in several other airmen. But what most oppressed them one and all was the mysterious nature of one of the fitters. They avoided both him and his glance, although he was a good chap and knew his job as well as anyone who had been in flying any length of time. Nearly a year previously it had been discovered that this mechanic possessed "second-sight," an ability to see into the future. At that time he had fore-warned two airmen several times in confidence that they would have to bale out, but they had not taken his advice and had crashed to their deaths. Some weeks afterwards this strange being had pointed at one of the pilots with the remark "He's next,"—and that pilot had in fact been the next to be killed. This last event had meant no rest for anyone—one and all mobbed the mechanic in their anxiety to find out who "the next" would be. The good man was clearly put out, and at first refused to answer; but they pressed him so closely that in the end he had come out with it. "Look after yourself carefully, Robert!" he told one of the airmen, "and not only you but . . ." then he had stopped short and stared a moment into the eyes of another until the man, who had blushed scarlet and whose pulse could be seen throbbing in the arteries of his throat, had looked away in confusion.

Robert had been killed, but the other one was still with us. This single mistake destroyed no one's faith, however, and the horror of receiving this kind of death sentence kept people from putting any more questions to their enigmatical, uncanny comrade. One or two of them had gone on trying to get him to talk when he had been drinking, but the old man since that day had kept silent. Nevertheless I knew I too would be going to him

32

before long, and in fact I was already turning over in my mind how I could best get his knowledge out of him.

"Immediate readiness!" resounded suddenly from the loudspeaker—*"Squadron take off at once!"*

We leapt into our machines and a minute later were already on our course. Close to Amiens the heavy bombers were roaring at five thousand metres. There were thirty of us, but in front were nearly a hundred four-engined aircraft, and high up in the blue firmament there might well be many times that number of fighters. Our engines were roaring at full throttle in our efforts to overtake the enemy formation and to get a few miles ahead of it. My engine was old and I had fallen astern. So I turned in sooner than the others to meet the bombers, whose pilots were to be our point of aim, and which we consequently had to attack from right ahead. I had in fact turned too soon on to this opposite course; my comrades, of whom I had been the rearmost, were suddenly a long way astern, a state of affairs which might be highly unpleasant, for the enemy would bring all his fire power to bear on me alone, the first isolated fighter to make his attack.

A heavy bomber was framed in my sights—looming larger every moment until it completely filled the sights. I fired, and the next moment it seemed I must collide with the giant before me. Kicking the rudder pedals with all my strength I thrust the stick forward with both hands, a trick which could be my salvation, for my aircraft plunged away vertically at the same speed as that with which I had gone into the attack. With a further kick and wrench I pulled it out of its dive. Behind me, innumerable smoke trails from the American's guns formed a protective wall, like a thundercloud with its storms of

33

hail and fringes of torn vapour. None of our aircraft **was** to be seen. The English fighters must have dived on them during the attack and broken up their formation— since I was alone I had not been noticed. I looked round anxiously for a comrade with whom I could join forces. Two American fighters were diving down from above —if I were to judge my aim well they would cross my line of fire. Just before the first burst I saw that they were German after all, but they were moving **very** fast and my own machine was too slow to overtake them.

A dark cloud of smoke stood out vertically in the sky. I flew close by it and my gaze followed it down to where it was belching with appalling force from the fuselage of a diving Spitfire. The fate of a life was being decided in these seconds, and I couldn't tear my eyes from the sight of the burning aircraft. I hoped—the thought tormented me—that the Englishman could still save himself by parachute, and at last the small white mushroom did open out against the dark landscape. Seeing his luck had gone the right way, I turned towards the airman to greet him and wish him well. I circled round the small, sprawling human figure below the parachute and waved across at him.

But as I look back before repeating this performance there are the roundels and gun-barrels again, glaring down at me from above. Spitfires! The fearful sight paralyses me. Their muzzles spit forth blazing steel and rake my aircraft fore and aft. It's as if a giant's fist has shaken us. I grasp the stick tightly, my heart has stopped and I can't breathe. Leaning forward, I stare at the instruments, and the delicate needles tremble in concert. They're swinging round together—the height indicator to the left, the speed to the right—that means I'm out of control. There! A hellish roar again as we shake afresh and I haul the stick back towards me. I hurtle vertically upwards—free! My left hand pushes the throttle right forward and the wounded bird twists upwards at full power into the sky. My head jerks round—the enemy's lying just astern of me with his guns still blazing. But his fire goes low as he follows my upward spiral—always that fraction of a second behind. I realise I'm automatically doing the right thing. Though the Englishman's engine may be the more powerful, the recoil of his guns is causing him to drop further and further behind. We climb more steeply still and the turns get tighter and tighter. Both of us are demanding the utmost from our aircraft, for the Tommy knows too that height must decide the outcome, that he who is finally above his opponent and can hunt him into the depths will win.

My flying suit is soaked right through with sweat, my hands slip wetly on the stick. Sweat runs warm into my eyes, over my nose and into the corners of my mouth.

"Stick it!" I say to myself. "Keep steady!"

I summon all my nervous energy in the struggle to gain every metre of height. Somebody once told me one must use the flaps to be able to combine the lowest speed with the greatest possible rate of climb. With misty eyes and trembling fingers I try to find the flap lever among the innumerable controls. The Englishman is still on my tail—but suddenly a German shows up just behind him.

"From Werner. Carry on turning! Don't dive away! I'm out of ammunition."

So it's Werner behind the Englishman, but without a bullet to help me with. I pull myself together and try

35

again to find the flap-lever. Instead I press the one next to it, and my machine drops. It looks like the end.

I glance back again quickly to where the enemy is climbing at me, with Werner just astern of him—within ramming distance. There's a gleam of hope the Tommy himself may look behind him and see there the gun-barrels of an unexpected opponent. But he doesn't do so and still tries to bring his guns to bear, never dreaming of the German just astern. So the Englishman draws slowly ahead. He has checked his fire and means to give me the *coup-de-grâce* at point-blank range. I fumble despairingly among the control levers, but my nerve has gone. I think I have pressed the right lever this time, but it's still the wrong one, and my aircraft drops once more. Too late! My nose dips sluggishly, and the machine falls. I am done for, and sit waiting for the enemy's burst, crouched numbly in the narrow cockpit. Let's hope the back armour will hold, flashes through my mind. I am still waiting. My limbs feel like lead, I can't bear to look while he shoots me down. But nothing happens. The clock's second hand is jerking inexorably round its circle close in front of my eyes. Blood, my own lifeblood, is singing in my ears with a shrill note like a violin-string, stretched beyond endurance—which must break—any moment—now.

"Shoot!" I scream. "Go on—shoot!" But still nothing happens.

A sudden violent noise in my earphones—I jerk my head around. Astern of me the Englishman, his airframe damaged, is spinning downward, with Werner gliding after in steep spirals.

"Rammed!" I hear his triumphant voice. "From Werner—Spitfire rammed!"

Only gradually I realize what has happened. His

heroic act has saved me: Werner has sliced off the tail of the Spitfire with his heavy propeller. I bring my aircraft under control again and dive towards him.

"Am attempting to land at Abbeville," Werner calls. "*Achtung!* Werner calling Abbeville. Request clear field. Landing without prop."

We glide slowly towards the Somme mouth, myself flying a few metres away from Werner, close behind him. His aircraft is in a very poor state. The propeller has gone, the engine-casing, cockpit-hood and wing-surfaces are badly bent and torn. A piece of metal—English metal—is caught up in the radio-mast. We are dropping lower and lower. Three thousand metres below us lies Abbeville airfield. We are approaching a flat layer of cloud. Werner tries to "land" on it, for he wants to see what is the lowest speed at which he will be able to land on the airfield when the time comes—at the moment the airflow breaks up and he can no longer keep his splintered aircraft under control. So he brings the machine into a stall a few yards above the cloud surface, and at a speed still little less than three hundred kilometres per hour it drops abruptly into the cotton-wool-like mist.

I dive in beside him.

"No use," Werner calls. "Landing's out of the question. I'm going to jump!" As we emerge from the cloud-bank I'm by his side once more. Then I turn clear as Werner throws off the cockpit-hood, releases his harness and stands up ready for jumping. I see him dragged from his seat, dashed against the fuselage and then falling—till the parachute silk billows out above his head. The abandoned machine has gone into a spin, which gets steeper and steeper until it finally dives vertically into the abyss.

Meanwhile Werner had found himself in a strange predicament. When he felt for the parachute release-handle he realized that the back-straps had slipped from his shoulders. So now his body was hanging horizontally in the air. But he would not be able to land in this position, for his back would be broken by the impact, since even with a parachute his fall would be equivalent to jumping from the first floor of a house.

Abruptly Werner broke into a laugh—his left arm was dangling uselessly towards the ground. He tried to draw it up towards him, but it was no use. It must have been dislocated when he crashed against the side of his aircraft. But all this didn't worry him overmuch, and in his present rôle of hovering angel he was able to enjoy the sight of the lovely world beneath him. But if at first he need only admire, soon a foreboding of evil crept up on him: his body was rotating, slowly but continuously. Gripping one of the back straps, he drew himself to a vertical position and looked upwards into the ballooning silk. Some of the cords connecting him with the parachute had parted, flapping clear of the white silk envelope, whose edge had turned itself up. The muscles of his extended, wrenched arm giving way, he carefully resumed his former horizontal position so as to husband all his strength for the moment of landing.

The slow rotations recommenced, and in a little while Werner shuddered to see that with each circle the parachute was becoming smaller. It seemed inevitable that in the end it would crash with him to earth in collapsed, useless folds! He had already seen that happen once at the flying school, when a man had jumped without a parachute. He had hit the ground only fifty metres away, bounced back several metres like a rubber doll and then subsided—so much dead pulp inside a flying suit. His

38

comrade's shriek, that awful shriek just before he struck, had been the worst thing of all. Werner had never forgotten it.

"No, not that!" he told himself with trembling lips, and once more hauled himself vertical with the whole strength of his one arm.

Werner looked down towards where the solid earth lay, an endless distance away, seeming never to get closer. My arm has got to hold out, he thought—I must hold myself upright! As he tried to raise his left hand again he realised at once that no strength remained in it: the hand hardly seemed to belong to him any more. The earth lay as far below him and as immobile as ever.

"I *must* do it!" he cried, as though in no other way could he force his body to do his will. With teeth clenched he counted the seconds till they drew into minutes. Nevertheless there were still about a thousand metres to be endured.

The fields seemed to move closer—a green surface across which flickered red spots and bright little stars. Werner's mouth was dry, his head burning and his hands clammy and stiff. He relapsed gradually into indifference to his fate. His will and his strength alike exhausted, the strap slipped slowly from his grip. It was as though he had fallen into a deep sleep. Once again he hung horizontally, while the parachute spun slowly and grew smaller still. Finally his eyes refused their duty and his pain and distress faded. He knew nothing more.

When he came to from his faint, the ground was scarcely a hundred metres away and coming sharply up to meet him. He hauled himself upright and raised his eyes. The parachute had become *very* small. Perhaps his legs would still be able to take the shock of landing—but how many men before him had hoped the same as they fell in their headlong plunge!

There just ahead, in front of the haystack, he would land in that meadow. He could see it still ahead as the ground struck him.

He lay for some minutes in the soft grass, utterly exhausted but joyful, though all his limbs were aching. With raw, stiff fingers he fumbled for a cigarette. Then he dragged himself to his feet.

CHAPTER IV

THE search party had already left before I landed. Scarcely an hour afterwards they rang up to say that Werner and his Tommy were safe and on their way back. But my Englishman had been taken to the Field Hospital severely wounded.

He's severely wounded, ran through my head. Pictures of the fight again came before my eyes—those seconds in which his parachute had opened. I had indeed waited for it to open. And yet my Tommy's wounded! It affected me just as if someone standing behind me had laid his hand on my arm, saying, "Now then, what sort of a chap are you! You've wounded me. Give me your explanation if you please!" What could I reply? That it's war? That we've got to shoot at one another so that the enemy can be destroyed? Or would you prefer me to play the part of a conqueror?

I felt the other would need a word from me: not of condescension, excuse or pity, but something that would show my recognition and respect. I cast around for something suitable and found it in my quarters: a bottle of "White Horse" whisky and a packet of "Navy Cut" which I had got from a man in U-boats.

My tread up the convent staircase was muffled by my flying-boots.

"You can't go in," whispered the orderly, "it's quite impossible. He's dying."

It was a shock—but then I pulled myself together. Still I hesitated a moment—perhaps indeed it wouldn't do for me to go in now.

"I want to see him all the same. Straight away!"

The orderly stood obstinately in my path before the small oak door. Then I pushed him to one side and went in.

A priest was leaning over the side of the iron bedstead. He seemed to have finished his office, to be waiting now to draw his hand over the eyes of the dying man. He looked at me in astonishment. But as I was still wearing my flying-suit, he might well have guessed what I wanted. As I stood there under the lintel of the door, my eyes came to rest on the pale features of the Englishman, the small young face of a nineteen-year-old. His eyes were closed. Perhaps he felt I was standing there, was only keeping his eyes closed because he did not want to see me, because he hated me. Around the corners of his mouth was playing a scarcely perceptible smile in which there lay a shade of bitterness and disappointment. His forehead was smooth below the parting of the fair hair.

Then he opened his eyes and gazed directly into mine.

I held myself under control and met his gaze. As he continued to stare at me, the black in the blue of his irises seemed to contract.

"You?" he said faintly. In that word there was horror and dread. It was only when I looked down at the sheet that I managed to reply "Yes, my friend."

His features relaxed afresh. "Come here," he said gently. The chaplain stood up and gave me his place.

"That's for you," I said, and sat down beside him. "Whisky and cigarettes."

"Let's have a look."

I took the paper wrapping from the bottle and showed him the cigarettes. His eyes rested on them for a while, and then they closed once more.

"White Horse and Navy Cut from Great Britain," I said deliberately, but with a cheerful undertone——

"Let's have a drink!" he began again, clearly this time, and opening his eyes. The priest nodded smilingly and went out with the bottle, returning a few minutes later to put the whisky to the lips of the dying man. I lifted my glass too.

"A cigarette."

I lit one for him, and put it between his lips. He drew the smoke in deeply, then breathed it out weakly, smiling now without bitterness or disappointment any longer. Then a shadow passed over the pale face, the eyelashes shifting slightly, the breath drawn gaspingly in. The waxen features were becoming rigid and cold. Only in the eyes life still flickered.

The priest was praying, and smiling at the same time, just like the dying man. Then he bent over the body, still smiling, and closed the eyes.

We walked back through the hospital.

"Thank you," said the chaplain. "You have made the great journey easier for him. Not every soldier has the chance of dying that way . . . if you understand. . . . I come from the East."

I nodded.

"People die rather differently there," he went on thoughtfully. "I have seen thousands go. At the end, during the retreat, I was at a field dressing station. They were bringing in dead and wounded—Russians and Germans alike, the surgeon amputating smashed and frozen legs and arms. The cold was terrible, the Russians were forcing us back with violent attacks. Every time we took to our sledges in panic we left a heap of arms and legs and whole corpses behind in the snow, and hundreds of men who had been operated on died on the open sledges as we hurried through the freezing night. Often the horses collapsed in their traces, and the wounded were then left to their fate, as the doctors were needed at the new positions. One of them shot himself when he found he was falling asleep time and time again during an operation and had three times amputated the legs of dead men. Today, however, I have once again had Friend Hein in cheerful mood—you know, there really is such a thing as 'dying pleasantly', when one's last thoughts are without a grudge, reconciled. . . ."

Werner had taken his captured Tommy to the mess. In accordance with custom he was told what other guests would be present, as we wanted to give this R.A.F. captain some help in getting through the first difficult hours in his new environment.

Our guest wore the ribbon of the Victoria Cross, which made us specially respect him. During our meal we had already discovered he had studied law in Heidelberg and spoke good German. He seemed more and more to want to forget his own misfortune and his comrade's and soon began to take a full part in our conversation.

Only Hinterschallers got a bit above himself when he said, "Herr Mister, do you know who rammed you?"

"Oh, yes, I have already had the honour of being introduced to my conqueror." With this the Englishman nodded towards Werner. "No doubt you belong to the élite of the German fighter pilots?"

"Not a bit of it!" Hinterschallers cried rudely. "He only flew with us for the first time to-day—complete beginner."

The Tommy became deathly pale. "It's inconceivable a beginner should have shot me down."

"I suppose that's why you're wearing a medal and are probably well-known in England," Hinterschallers commented unpleasantly.

The Squadron Commander was just about to intervene when the man from the "other field post number" laughed and pointed to his ribbon: "Oh, that's just a medal for long service. I also was making my first operational flight to-day. But once has been quite enough, I'm glad I shan't have to fight any more."

"Hinterschallers!" our chief called, reckoning things had gone far enough. "Go and pull on the beam and bring me the latest *Interavia*!"

The Mess Sergeant went sullenly to the door where the cord of the "Lying-beam" was fastened, and pulled. We looked with amusement up towards the lamp below which was a rafter with a concealed hinge. Now it was bent in the middle.

"My invention, too," Hinterschallers muttered as he left the room.

"Oh," cried the Tommy delightedly, "what a grand idea! If the beam bends someone here has told a tall one. But that means you, because certainly no beginner ever shot *me* down!"

"But you say you have only been in action for the first time to-day!" several of us came back, though we knew quite well he himself had lied out of shame. The Tommy only nodded—but it wasn't convincing.

Hinterschallers had meanwhile brought the *Interavia*, the international air periodical which the Englishman also knew well.

"Have a look here," our Kapitän invited him, turning to a page which showed photographs of the latest German and Allied flying aces. "You see, Captain, here you are with the Victoria Cross and here am I too, only with us it's the *Ritterkreuz*!"

At this our guest could no longer hide his embarrassment. "Oh yes," he said. "I'm sorry, we always get the *Interavia* much later than you do."

Then he broke into hearty laughter and we with him.

"Well, are we quits now for tall stories?" the Chief asked, raising his glass.

"Prost!" cried Tommy. "Quits among friends!"

Around midnight, when most of the others had gone to bed, Hinterschallers still stayed on in the mess. Again and yet again he filled up his own and the Englishman's glass, describing in a mixture of German and English, Latin and French the qualities of a digestive preparation which he, Hinterschallers, manufactured and purveyed in peacetime. His combination of philosophy and digestive tablets culminated with the Tommy actually shaking Hinterschallers's hand. Touched in his heart and stomach.

"Good," he promised, "I agree to take over the London representation of your firm. I'll fly back to-morrow."

CHAPTER V

THE Squadron Commander opened the morning conference with, "To-day we've got a bit of a procession. Two machines take off at 9.45. Object: observation of enemy activity in the harbours of Dover and Folkestone. A sharp look-out is to be kept for any possible assembly of invasion shipping. Approach as usual: along the coast at nought feet to Cap Grisnez and then across to Dover and Folkestone. On the return journey keep your eyes skinned! Spitfires will certainly be on the lookout for us. It's best to fly back over Cap Grisnez. So—now let's draw lots."

One of the senior pilots and I were the ones to draw the shortest matches.

I took with me an additional yellow-coloured bag and Pervitin. One never knew. Generally speaking, either both or neither came back from these armed reconnaissance flights, and water is not an airman's element.

For quite a time already the British captain had been standing on the wing of my aircraft, studying the cockpit lay-out. He was still treated as our guest till whenever he should be taken away to the transit camp for all Allied pilots at Oberursel.

"Hello, Captain, I'm just off to have a look across the Channel. Coming too?"

The other smiled sourly. "I thought I told you yesterday I'm glad to have the war behind me. I won't be flying any more. Tell me," he added after a pause, "rather

47

cramped in here, isn't it? It interests me simply from a
technical point of view."

He swung himself into the pilot's seat. I left him alone
and went off to report myself out. As a precaution I had
placed the chocks in front of the wheels.

The Kapitän laughed: "He takes us for fools. He's an
optimist all right." At that moment we heard the starter
whining.

"He's trying to take off!" an excited shout came from
the mechanics. I sprang towards the machine. The
propeller was already turning slowly with the motor
started up—at full throttle. The slipstream blew me to
the ground—but, the machine straining against the
chocks, it was hopeless to try and take off.

When the Englishman saw how it was he cut his
throttle. I climbed up to him, for in any case it was time
for me to take off. The Captain was crouching in the
cockpit, disappointed and broken. He seemed to have
shrunk into himself, and his face looked old and flat.

"Come out, Captain, I've got to get off!"

He groaned. "The chocks! I never noticed them."

A short while later we were flying northwards, staying
close to the ground so that the English radar on the other
side of the Channel should not pick us up. We shot
purposefully over ploughed fields and woods, villages
and streets. Far behind in the west and north shimmered
the sea. A dot showed up in the field before us—a
peasant walking composedly beside two horses, a man
who heard the noise of our engines, a man with both his
feet on the ground who was holding his animals firmly
by their harness and didn't know whether we might not
be an enemy. We hurtled like lightning over his land,
flashing above him like the crack of a whip. A quick look
back—the peasant was still clinging to his horses which

were panicking and trying to bolt. Then a farm, and again ploughed fields, meadows and a thousand painted landscapes.

We would only have needed to pull back the stick for a second and all these bright objects—so close we could almost touch them—would have merged simply into markings on a map. The high ground of Artois rose out of the plain and a monument drew past us like a threatening finger. The conical slag heaps of the coal mines towered above our heads, and soon we were roaring over Grisnez.

A birch wood, a small cliff, sand, barbed wire and frothing surf: here the continent ended, green land divided by blue water from the island lying such a short distance away. Our machines danced nimbly across the shore and over the sea, whose waves licked at us greedily. Now, at this narrowest point of the Channel, we must save all the time we could. We must fly the thirty-two kilometres across in the shortest possible time and we needed two hundred seconds to get us to the opposite shore. We were almost touching the white horses, the spray beating against our fuselage. Grisnez sank away further and further behind us and in fact we would have to fly even lower if we were not to be picked up in England.

Across the other side there gleamed a golden-white line: the cliffs, in which hundreds of guns lay in wait. Perhaps they had already spotted us and were expecting us? The harbour works of Dover grew larger and now lay clearly visible ahead.

All of a sudden flashes started up from every corner, and innumerable projectiles hurtled towards us, for all the world as if they were tied to the ends of strings. We hauled up into the sky and turned back—Dover harbour was empty. The lines of tracer were falling well astern as

we swung in towards Folkestone. There there was one
M.T.B. only, just entering harbour.

Our job done now, we turned back towards Grisnez.
I kept peering around me, as the Spitfires must have
taken off by now. We were flying at maximum revs,
forcing our aircraft down lower and closing our engine-
gills. I looked across at my comrade. His aircraft was
steady as a rock in the air, but the engine seemed to be
over-oiling, as a dark plume of smoke lay astern of him.
The next moment it burst into flames!

"You're on fire!" I cried. But the other had already
released his cockpit hood and swung himself out of his
seat.

While my companion drifted above the sea in his parachute I passed an S O S over my radio and reported the
position. Then I circled above the spot where he had
jumped and tried to estimate how far he was from land.
He was lying exactly in mid-Channel. I flew as low, as
close and as slowly as possible over the small rubber boat
as it danced among the waves: the poor chap down there
was hauling himself laboriously into it. A slow yellow
stain spread outwards from the colour-bag until a great
yellow patch indicated the position of the accident clearly
to a considerable distance away.

"*Look out for Spitfires!*" I heard in my earphones. It
was the ground-station giving me warning.

I glanced quickly towards England, and there they
were, two—five—nine small dots drawing ever closer.
There was no point in my staying any longer, as I couldn't
help any more. So I headed towards the coast, setting my
course again for Grisnez.

The crash might well have been seen from both sides
of the Channel, and in fact a race started from island and
continent simultaneously. Some infantrymen had launched

an assault-craft and started across the Channel, while a British M.T.B. dashed out at full-speed towards the spot.

A flight of German fighters, whose unit must have been stationed close to the shore, came to meet me over Grisnez. They had clearly been sent off for an emergency search, so I joined up with them and led the four aircraft towards the scene of the accident.

The British were already circling above the spot, although beneath us on the water the Germans seemed to have been the first to get there. A stiff fight now developed round the boats: we attacking the M.T.B. and the Tommies our assault-craft. Soon we joined battle with one another in the air. In the end two Germans and two Englishmen were parachuting down—the price of saving one individual from the sea! The M.T.B. turned away and our own rescuing boat had capsized. . . .

The red warning-lamp of my petrol-gauge was glowing —in twenty minutes I would have to land somewhere. I disengaged, and ten minutes later came to rest on a small advanced airfield near the coast.

Our "search-flights" were taking off every hour in rotation as the five airmen and three assault-pioneers were still swimming about in the sea. It was only in the after-noon, when it became more misty over the water, that the M.T.B. ventured again to approach our own and the enemy swimmers and to pick them up, under strong Spitfire escort. The last German *Schwarm* gave in to such superior forces but we were consoled by the fact that at any rate all the men had been saved.

I had joined up with another four aircraft of the neighbouring squadron in order to get back to Abbeville. The mist had become so thick that visibility was reduced to two or three kilometres, and soon we were flying in thick fog. One could still just see the next aircraft. This change of weather had come down too suddenly for us to be able to turn back. In any case, the fog might well extend on a broad front over the whole countryside.

"We'll climb above it," ordered the *Schwarmführer*.

The "fly" raised itself gently above the artificial horizon, the compass swung slowly, the needle of the air-speed indicator fell back scarcely perceptibly and the altimeter registered a steady gain in height. My eyes swung periodically from the instruments across to the next aircraft and then ahead into the fog. We were flying slowly, at half-throttle, the altimeter now recording three hundred metres. The danger seemed to have passed, for the highest points in the Artois hills now lay a hundred metres below us.

At this moment something slid away from beneath me. Instinctively I pulled the stick back towards me as a green wall suddenly appeared right ahead—and then disappeared. The altimeter jumped upwards and the needle of the air-speed indicator fell back heavily. I opened the throttle wide, not knowing whether I was lying on my back or pointing vertically upwards into the air. The next moment it grew light—the sun was shining in the west and the treacherous cotton-wool lay beneath me.

Having brought my aircraft back to normal flying position, I proceeded to call up my comrades. But there was no answer. Instead, the ground-station reported "All airfields in thick fog. Abbeville: ground-mist up to thirty metres. Bale out if necessary!" I flew to the Somme mouth by compass and stop-watch. I hadn't much time left, as the tank would be empty in ten minutes.

The ground station called me up once more. "*You are directly above us. Do you want to land?*"

"I'll try," I passed back. And there was the Abbeville church steeple piercing through the milk soup. "I am making my approach over the church steeple and will hold off just above the fog surface. When you hear me over the south edge of the airfield, call me up!"

I almost touched the weather-cock on the tower, I came in so low. My wheels trailing through cotton-wool, I approached the edge of the airfield at two hundred kilometres an hour. I throttled back more and more, and the needle stayed poised at 190.

"*You're coming straight towards us,*" came up over the radio. "*Cut your throttle.*" I drew the throttle-lever right home and pulled the stick cautiously and gently back towards me. My eyes were glued to the artificial horizon, the air-speed indicator and the variometer: the machine must lie exactly on the "horizon," the speed must not drop below 180 and the variometer showed me that the aircraft was dropping at the rate of a metre a second—I hovered in mid-air, it seemed for an eternity, though really it was for seconds only. Nothing moved, the lead-coloured vapour lying numb and dead all around me, the instruments alone still telling me I had not yet landed. I was afraid of overshooting the airfield and hitting one of the hangars, and I felt even worse as it seemed the ground was simply not there.

I was just on the point of opening the throttle and taking off again when the undercarriage struck heavily. As I braked sharply left and right alternately, a hangar loomed up in front of me, rushing to meet me out of the mist, with mechanics running clear. Once again I stamped with all my strength on the brakes—the aircraft groaned, sank forward almost on to its knees—but did not turn over.

My single-seater had come to rest a few steps away

from the hangar—its wheels and brakes smoking. And before I could switch it off, the engine petered out—the last drop of petrol had been used up.

The last night-sentries were being relieved on the other side of the world, for a short rest till they should be awakened to a morning of fresh slaughter, while in Europe soldiers made ready for the ending of their day, and people in cities waited for the bombs. For our part we were waiting for one of our comrades to land, the superstitious one who never flew without his small piece of wood. Despite his three-fold tapping he had come down somewhere that very morning with engine trouble and had rung up to report that he would get back to us before nightfall. The fog had dispersed as suddenly as it had come down, and by our reckoning our friend should have landed long since. Indeed now that dusk had overtaken us, colours fading and the outlines of everything becoming more and more indistinct till they finally merged into a grey mass, he had clearly lost his way. Radio waves alone connected him with us—alternately speaking and listening. By this means he could discuss with us what to do, asking whether we had yet picked up the noise of his engine. In reply he was told to fly in squares of ever-increasing size, as in this way he must inevitably come somewhere near us.

Scarcely five minutes went by before we heard the hum of his engine far off, quite soft, then louder, and then again growing less. He was told to alter course at once to the left. In this way he got continually closer till he could see our signals—Very lights and coloured rockets being fired without a break into the air. Meanwhile fire-engine and ambulance were standing by to dash to the spot in the event of an accident, and red and white lights glowing everywhere to help him make his unaccustomed night landing.

The machine slipped in only a few feet above our heads, touched down, turned over and—burst into flames.

As, a few seconds later, we stood round the heap of wreckage, it already looked as if nothing could be saved. The tank had emptied and the aircraft was lying on its back in a wide pool of flaming petrol. Struggle as the firemen might, they couldn't get the blaze under control.

"He's still alive!" someone shouted, and the words struck home, for at that moment our trapped comrade's horrible screaming came through to us, muffled by the closed cockpit-hood and drowned by the crackling of the flames.

A human being burning alive before our eyes! At intervals we could make out the condemned man writhing and jerking convulsively—hammering on the unyielding walls of his glass cage, every moment more and more enveloped by the roaring flames.

"Won't anyone help him?" a senior fireman shouted. His despairing cry made us all realize simultaneously the only thing which could be done to ease our comrade's torment—given a careful marksman, a single pistol-shot would be enough.

But then there was the awful fear of perhaps not killing the unfortunate man outright, not to speak of such conduct not being upheld as justified by the subsequent court-martial. Besides, mightn't it even be our own unsure consciences that stopped us putting an end to a friend's terrible sufferings? Meanwhile the burning man was still shrieking and writhing—several of the bystanders had turned away so as not to see the dreadful sight.

At that moment Ulrich leaped forward up to the flames, raised his revolver and took steady aim at the pilot's head.

"Halt!" An officer called him back. "You can't do that! Don't you know what you're doing?"

Ulrich turned on him sharply, but the other seized him by the arm. "You don't know what comes after death!"

"Certainly nothing worse than what's happening here!" Ulrich shouted back, loud enough for us all to hear, and shook the other off. The next minute his shot rang out.

On our unhappy way home we saw that Ulrich's hair had been singed by the heat, so close had he had to stand so as not to miss his friend's head.

After that we drank a good deal, to forget it all. It had been a day of extremes. The B.B.C. moaned on hour by hour, without our having to pay for it. Everyone made an awful din and Ulrich bawled loudest of all, laughed, danced or just lay apathetically in his arm-chair. We wanted to forget—just to forget.

Those who got drunk staggered one by one to their quarters or lay about dishevelled and snoring on the cushions. And the B.B.C.'s insipid jazz droned monotonously on.

CHAPTER VI

"THAT'S the new cadet-pilot," my mechanic called across to me. The new man had only been casually introduced. Now he was roaring away close over our heads and waggling his wings in token of his first victory in combat.

"What's his name?"

"They call him George," said the mechanic, moving discreetly away.

Shortly afterwards George clambered from his machine. His fresh face was red from the heat of battle and his eyes shifted rapidly from one object to another. When he made his report it was plainly hard for him to talk quietly and with self-possession. Afterwards as he told his story to the pilots who thronged around him, his hands helped him to illustrate the course of the fight. He was even able to describe exactly the state of the enemy aircraft when it was shot down.

When his first excitement had subsided, George's thoughts moved on into the private realm of his secret longings, which he had been ashamed to tell the others. I forgave him for that, for I could guess them easily enough—the first was surely that the Kommandeur would pin the Iron Cross on his chest—perhaps he would get accelerated promotion, indeed if he went on being as successful as this the possibility of greater distinction could not be ruled out—then there would be some leave—

just after his getting his commission, of course—he didn't want to go home until *that* had happened!

As I watched him pretty closely I could be fairly certain my guess was correct. Who could blame a cadet for counting the hours until his decoration, for staking everything on getting some recognition of his courage, an outward sign of his personal bravery to brand him an established member of the fighting fraternity, to bring him honour, fame and respect, and distinguish him even among the brave? I couldn't help thinking of the tens of thousands of cadets of all nations, who were either fighting one another or waiting for a chance to fight to defend their own and so distinguish themselves as knights of this noble order. These young men differed so little from each other, forming as they did an international caste of uniform habits of mind and uniform objectives—unspoilt idealists, strict in their inward discipline and outward control. Convinced of the rightness of all they were defending, brave and self-sacrificing fighters, they were the officers of the future, destined to occupy the most responsible, often the highest, positions in the public eye. Their path was a straight one, admitting no compromise—in which they differed from other men.

The telephone rang.

It was for George, into whose world of dreams I had been peering. The Kommandeur wished to speak to him, and George reported himself in a firm voice.

A few minutes later I witnessed an outburst of utter despair . . . our cadet was back and sitting by me with his head and arms on the table. He was weeping—weeping for the airman whom he had shot down and killed scarcely an hour previously; for he had shot down one of his own comrades.

George failed to appear at lunch, and crept away in

the afternoon to where no one could find him. Everyone knew that a court-martial would have to pronounce sentence on him next day. Finally the Kapitän had sent for him.

"You will take off for Lille in ten minutes. The Kommandeur wants to ask you some questions personally. I'm coming with you."

As the two aircraft taxied towards the take-off, they looked like two broken-winged hornets crawling along. The cadet was keeping just astern of his chief, but all of a sudden the Kapitän's aircraft came to a halt with George still moving up close behind him. We hoped he would see the Kapitän in time, but George couldn't see anything, as his big engine completely cut off his view ahead.

We saw it coming, clenched our fists and shouted warnings at the top of our voices. But George couldn't hear. Only another few seconds . . . and then a crash, a shriek, and quiet once more.

We leaped into the car.

George was climbing down from the cockpit. Something was still humming in the wreckage. A piece of metal crackled softly. The dead Kapitän was scarcely recognizable in the mass of crumpled metal that had been his machine: red pulped flesh and bloodstained tufts of hair. The heavy propeller had hacked and mashed him to slivers.

George walked away, dragging himself across the airfield. We wanted to take him with us in the car but he just looked at us once in a lost fashion, murmuring something about "ramming".

Firemen and medical orderlies were standing round, but there was no work for them to do.

We drove silently back to squadron.

"Where's he gone?" someone said at last. We all looked across the airfield.

"He's going to the Kommandeur's quarters."

"And now he's running!" Ulrich cried.

Yes, George was running all right—running faster and faster. We quite understood. No one must get there ahead of him, for no one had a greater right to accuse him than himself.

The pilots were standing dumbly about in front of their easy-chairs. We knew George was still running. But no one wanted to look and they all felt that they shouldn't sit down while their comrade was running like that.

Our good old Welfare Officer, Papi, whose job it was to deal with all such emotional crises, came up. He looked across the field to where George must still be on his way.

"He's going to report to the Kommandeur," I said. Papi nodded and drew me aside.

"It's all too much for the youngster," he began after a while. "I ought to have anticipated this second business, and told the Kommandeur. What shall I do now?" He stared vacantly in front of him. Though in the past he had been able to help many of us, now he subsided helplessly into his easy-chair. "I want to help, but I can't. I just can't do any more!" His face crumpled.

He hadn't been able to help his own son, who had stayed in Stalingrad. And he could give no aid to George, who was already accusing himself before the Kommandeur.

Poor Papi, he couldn't really help any of the people who received his letters. Every night he sat in torment at his desk, hurt by every line he had to write to the mothers, wives and fiancées of men who had just been killed. Letters to people who had lost their best and dearest unexpectedly, irrevocably. Letters, indeed, each of which was a kind of sealed death-sentence—how much more unfair, precise and unexpected than a sentence on the guilty. . . .

One letter Papi handed me was from a father, a gallant pensioner from the First World War. It concerned his youngest son, one of our pilots. At the beginning of the letter he described in some embarrassment his poor domestic circumstances . . . "my hand is more at home with a spade than with a pen," and ". . . it shouldn't really be me writing to you, but, you see, my wife is no longer alive." The sacrifice of his youth and strength in the First World War completed for me a picture of the old man, an honourable, industrious father, always concerned for the welfare of his family, as he had been for his country. It had clearly been very difficult for him, whose life had been one of modesty and discretion, to go against his principles by writing this letter. Only the greatest need could have impelled him to do so, as all his sons except the youngest, our comrade, had fallen on the field of battle. The mother of these young men had prayed for this last child of hers, torn between her mourning and her hope, until the burden of anxiety had become too great for her to bear. Now the old father was alone, and was asking, in his awkward fashion, for his last child to be sent back to him.

"How *can* I write and tell him that his son, the last child, is dead too?" Papi looked at me hopelessly. "How can I say that his son was shot down in error by one of his own squadron?"

I tried to evade the point. "Still, perhaps it's worse for George than it is for the father."

"Yes, I think George would rather have been killed himself than have caused this double tragedy. Of course, he'll be grounded for it."

"He murmured something about 'ramming,'" I added, hesitating.

"Ramming?" Papi repeated.

"He won't have much of a chance of that, from now on."

"He deserves a chance," the old officer answered firmly as he walked away.

CHAPTER VII

A WIDE belt of high pressure was moving in from the Atlantic, which Ulrich called a "mammoth high." The good men in the Condors had discovered it. In their four-engined aircraft they had flown thousands of kilometres over the sea between the Azores and Iceland, taking off in Southern France, and only touching down again when they reached Norway. A short while afterwards our "weather-frogs" had received a radio message from them which was to mean death for several of us.

For the following day was going to be clear. There would be no clouds into which we could dive when the enemy air superiority became too great. The Spitfires would dive on us out of the sun, as they always did in clear weather, out of its dazzling, blinding ball, while the Boeings and Lancasters assembled in their hundreds over England to bomb our cities.

To top everything, an "Order of the Führer" arrived in the evening. Our combat successes had, it seemed, been too few. Four-engined bombers were now no longer to be attacked from right ahead on opposite courses, but from positions astern. Only we knew what that meant. A single attack would now last thirty seconds, and not three as formerly. The concentrated fire of the enemy would spray us for half a minute with bullets, for which period we would be without protection or concealment— a long time, probably too long, for us to have a chance of emerging alive. Instead of approaching our target at 250 metres per second, we would have to overhaul the enemy gradually from astern, as the bombers flew only a little more slowly than ourselves. The enemy pilots would no longer have to look down our gun-barrels, but we, on the other hand, would have to make our approach under the eyes of the rear-gunners and in the face of hundreds of weapons for long enough for them to shoot us down before we could even fire our first burst.

Well, we had taken an oath, which made it easier to carry out our new instructions.

When the ominously fine weather arrived we were still fast asleep despite all our uneasy premonitions of the coming fight.

As on every morning, we sat waiting in our easy-chairs, ready to take off at any moment. This waiting was the worst thing of all. However much was talked, our ears and thoughts were inevitably trained on the loud-speaker, in continual expectation of a report of approaching enemy aircraft, of the order to take off. It was hard on the nerves. Already I had been twice to the lavatory, and others had been more than that.

Something in the loud-speaker went crack: it was an electrician carrying out a test. But several fellows sprang to their feet and turned towards the noise, their faces tense. One of the older men vomited—he had already flown himself out at twenty-three. Most of them pulled automatically at their cigarettes, threw them away half smoked, with nervy, irritable movements, only to light fresh ones. The mishaps of the previous day together with our impending operation, which looked like virtual suicide, had combined to make an insupportable atmosphere.

64

Only Ulrich sat beside me as usual, writing away at something which he wouldn't let anyone even glance at. But now he laid his pencil aside.

"I've finished," he grinned. Getting to his feet, he took up a position in front of the line of men and began an imitation of "fat Hermann."

"Comrades of the Luftwaffe! For the strengthening of morale, for the improvement of the offensive spirit, training and discipline of my troops, I consider it necessary to read publicly Routine Order number LDv 217 stroke c, part A."

Everyone was struck dumb, we all looked at him malevolently. This was simply too grotesque, too painful. With the bloodstained wreckage of the recent disaster still on the ground a few hundred metres away, and the court-martial already gathering in the barracks opposite to pass sentence on the youngest of the squadron, with the pilots waiting here in their easy-chairs with their nerves keyed up for their most difficult operation hitherto, here was Ulrich giving us a bit of music-hall a damn side too close to the bone. I was in the act of jumping up to stop him when Papi restrained me.

"Let him be. He's all right, I know what he's after." Slowly I began to understand. Ulrich wanted to break the spell which was lying over us all, to make us laugh just once before we jumped into our machines. We needed a shock of some sort to ease our physical and spiritual cramp. Still no one had spoken—a single word would be enough to start a row—and still Ulrich stood there before us, in full control of himself and very conscious of this possibility. I sensed his inward struggle, for the burden of the day which had passed, and of the operation which impended, bore down just as heavily on him. But now that he had started something he must pull it off. He simply had to make us laugh—before someone jumped up to knock him down.

Ulrich summoned all his strength. Noisily clearing his throat and with his left foot majestically forward, he carried on in good voice:

"Part A: Action Stations. At the order 'Action Stations' pilots will proceed at a steady double to their aircraft. The pilot and No. 1 mechanic will fall in facing one another three paces in front of the right trailing-edge of the left wing and take up the ground position. The pilot will apply his right hand to his headgear and report, 'Pilot ready for take-off!' The No. 1 mechanic will thereupon apply his right hand to his headgear, or in the event of none being available, will raise his right arm in the German salute (also see LDv 28 stroke 2b, page 83, para. 4) and report, 'Nothing fresh to report concerning the machine!' The two will then change places, as for guard-relief, with the words 'Machine handed over correct!' and 'Machine taken over correct!' The pilot will then proceed at a short, quick step to the left side of the aircraft facing the cabin and will take up the ground position. The right hand will grasp the upper foothold with the thumb extended along the lower edge. The right leg will be drawn up with the knee bent as close to the body as possible and the foot placed on the lower foot-rest. The pilot will push himself off with the ball of the left foot and pull himself upwards on to the wing. With a short, rhythmical movement he will then swing himself into the cockpit."

He paused for breath. The situation was practically in hand, the joke being gradually accepted. The chaps were listening, some smiling, some shaking their heads, some just looking at the ground but nevertheless intrigued by such an outrageous representation of something they were always having to do with the extreme of speed and tension: Meanwhile Ulrich's declamation proceeded:

"The harness will be fastened in the following sequence:

Upper lifeboat-strap
Lower lifeboat-strap
Left lower parachute-strap
Right lower parachute-strap
Left upper parachute-strap
Right upper parachute-strap
Left belly-strap
Right belly-strap
Left shoulder-strap
Right shoulder-strap.

If the correct sequence should be missed the process will be repeated from the start."

Vogel, Meyer II and I burst into laughter at this absurdity, and most of the others joined in. Ulrich was winning. At this moment came the first report.

"Achtung! Large formations, probably bombers, assembling over London.—Take-off is likely in ten minutes' time."

We who knew what it meant shivered as though frozen. Ulrich continued inexorably:

"Part B: Take-off. At the order 'Take-off' the pilot will adjust his mental attitude with a jerk to align it with the forthcoming combat. While doing this the head will remain still. The weight of the body will at the same time be equally distributed on both buttocks. The face will take up its characteristic expression and the eyes will be directed straight ahead with the chin thrust forward. The engine will then be started in accordance with LDv 763 stroke a, part 6b, page 24, section 3, para. 1."

The tense atmosphere had finally broken, and everyone laughed and clamoured for him to continue. They scarcely listened any longer to the reported positions of the enemy formation.

"Part C: Attack. If the enemy is sighted, the order 'Load and on safety-catch!' will be given. The firing position will be taken up, the safety-catch adjusted with the outstretched index-finger of the left hand, the left eye will be closed and the enemy held firmly in the sights with the right eye. The right index-finger will be pressed against the trigger-guard. On the word 'Fire' the enemy is to be shot down. After shooting-down: eyes up, finger extended, head raised, and stick quietly released. Should, however, flak be encountered during the air battle the duty of the fighter is fulfilled, for the enemy can only anticipate a quick and awful end.

"Part D: Attack by the enemy. On approaching an enemy, some such intention will be anticipated. On nearer approach, course will be altered downwards. Junior pilots will report by radio-telephone in the following words, 'Please, Herr Formation-leader, may I go home?'

"Part E: Emergencies. Shot down pilots will assemble on the ground and will be led home by the senior airman present. In these circumstances, movement across the terrain and singing will be carried out in accordance with the Manual of Infantry Training. On reaching a first, second or third-class road the senior airman will form the pilots into column of route and lead them to shelter, singing songs of the fatherland while so doing."

We jumped laughing into our aircraft, some of us in accordance with LDv 217. The spell had been broken.

"*Bombers proceeding towards the mouth of the Scheldt, height 7,000 metres.*"

Sixty engines started up all round the broad airfield as the order was given to take off.

The dispersal points of the four squadrons lay in the

form of a square, so that their take-off paths crossed each other. This unavoidable crossing-over was very danger-ous, as at the centre of the field, with one's nose slightly up, it was impossible to see across to the opposite side, and collisions during take-off had hitherto mostly been fatal. So we waited for the red Very light which would give us our all-clear signal once our opposite number had taken off.

As the first machines passed on their way above our heads and the red light shone out, we pressed the throttle-lever forward and roared away with only a few metres to spare between us on either side. The eighty-hundred-weight aircraft rose laboriously from the ground, the air-speed indicator showing 180 Kms.

Something was slipping towards us from our left front. I heard a muffled report and there was a glare of light, but there was no time yet to look round, though I noticed as I climbed that one of our neighbours was no longer in formation.

It was only during the circuit of the great airfield that I made out the mushroom of smoke and the blazing wreck-age that meant a collision, but I managed to look calmly on at it, for I had become increasingly indifferent as time went by. Who was to say whether both of them would not have fallen in combat an hour afterwards? However, they certainly ought to give the Very pistol to people a little more aware of their responsibility.

Below and astern I saw a single aircraft, climbing towards us. George, I thought—but, of course, the Kammandeur had forbidden him to fly.

We climbed quickly to 7,000 metres, and Belgium and Northern France already lying astern, a formation of sixty German fighters flying into battle, a fine and uncommon sight.

Fresh instructions were still coming over the radio from the ground station. Apparently the enemy was already on the return journey and now lay over Flushing.

"Break off and fly home!" we heard a moment later, followed by, "*No—don't be deceived! This is Headquarters. The Tommies are passing in false instructions. Fly on to Flushing!*"

An English transmitter had been tuned in on our frequency, the operator giving misleading orders and cleverly imitating our ground-controller's voice.

"No, this is your Headquarters, men," the same fellow cried again. "To the Kommandeur. Fly Garden-fence and make for Havana!" These fellows even knew our secret code for orders to land. But the voice was still not quite that of our Commanding Officer. The British espionage service in general worked exceedingly well, even knowing the names of our pilots, how old they were, how many aircraft they had shot down and when they were promoted.

"*Climb to 8,000 metres! Bombers now in the middle of the Channel.*" But the report was wrong—the enemy had interfered with our direction-finding sets on the ground and had produced an artificial echo by dropping strips of silver-paper.

"There they are, right ahead!" someone called abruptly in our earphones. Yes—there they *were*. At 6,000 metres and still over the land. Those are they, the stumpy objects suspended over there in the sky. Four-engined bombers—Boeings! And many more small dots above them. Spitfires and Thunderbolts—in all, probably several hundred.

A constructor saw them first—one of the many trying to find out by experiment some miraculous means of dealing with these formidable four-engined bombers.

This time he has suspended a bomb beneath his fuselage which he's going to launch at the end of a wire.

He's flying ahead now, so as to bring his new invention into action. Choosing the leading bomber, he flies above it at a distance of 200 metres and pays out his bomb ahead of the monster.

But he's being fired at. He's brought down, and an exploding Boeing with him—the bomb has hit.

Now we're in the thick of it ourselves. Full throttle and aim!

A dark shape with American markings is hanging in the sky before me.

"I must hit—must hit," I stammer to myself—and then, "Don't let me be hit! Don't hit *me*!" I don't see any enemy fire. Perhaps you only see it for the first time when it hits!

My red bursts of fire tear into the body of the bomber and rake him. I hope the rear-gunner's dead. If only I can hit the pilot!

These are my dearest wishes.

The colossus I am closing in on from astern grows larger and larger, until he is hanging, gigantic, scarcely fifty metres bang ahead! His slipstream tosses my little aircraft like a child's ball this way and that. But my guns are still firing whenever the black coffin comes into my sights.

There he goes! He lurches, then rears up like a stricken giant. The pilot *must* have been hit.

Slowly and ponderously the great mass starts to tip over, then goes into a spin—steeper and swifter each moment. I count seven parachutes.

Now the next bomber's ahead of me. You get so worked up, and if the whole business weren't so dangerous it could even be sport. You almost get to long for it, in

71

the throes of your lustful fever for the chase! Now fire at
his engines! One of them is already on fire, a dirty yellow
smoke-garland trailing away astern.

The fighters are diving down from all directions on to
their prey—trying to think of them as beasts who trample
women and children under their hooves.

Down with this one now!

The remaining engines are beginning to burn. From
the side comes one of our own men, right across my line
of fire—I check for a moment—and he's through.

It's utter uproar on the radio, everyone calling everyone else, cursing hoarsely or passing warnings. Every
now and again someone cries out in despair as he spins
away in flames. I have no time to do much thinking,
or to dwell on other people's fate. Everyone must look
after himself.

Someone shouts, "I'm going to ram!"

A scream—"That's George!"

Pieces of wreckage are falling through the air. George
has hurled his aircraft straight at the hull of the Boeing,
and friend and foe reel down earthwards together.

Well—he's redeemed himself all right.

I've been hit somewhere. That's what happens once
you start sentimentalizing. I turn away sharply. You
can only die once. What's more, I'm quite exhausted,
the sweat pouring through my eyebrows. My hands are
trembling as my eyes search wildly all around: everywhere
the sight of aircraft falling from the sky meets them,
everywhere dark smoke-trails, yellow flames and white
parachutes—while far below lies the blue Channel. How
wonderful it would be to fly home peacefully—now! To
get away from this mass-grave, the dead men beside me,
above and below me. No one would notice if I were to
break away and fly back.

But over there are still more four-engined aircraft. With the thought of bombs dropped on our homeland, of the oath I took as a seventeen-year-old, I fling myself once more at the stern of those grey shapes, those dispensers of multifarious death. Once again the clumsy Boeings slide away from in front of me, trailing their dark smoke, like wounded insects crawling away to shelter. My machine flies right into the thick smoke lying astern of them which now covers my approach.

The gaps in the enemy formations are getting larger. I can still only see isolated German fighters.

I'm just turning into my fifth attack when a Thunderbolt appears in the air a few metres to one side of me, out of which a negro's face is staring at me in horror. He's flying into the defensive fire of his own bomber! I take up a position scarcely thirty metres astern of him. But my guns are not firing. Wrench furiously as I may at all the knobs and levers, it's no use. My ammunition is expended.

I dive away vertically downward and force my head round to look. Is that negro after me? The needle of the air-speed indicator moves steadily across the dial: 600—700—750—800, and my aircraft rotates slowly on its long axis. When I look slightly upwards quite a part of Europe is displayed in front of me as though on a merry-go-round: Belgium—the Channel—England—the Channel again—Holland—Belgium—and once more the Channel. The dial now shows well over 800 kilometres an hour, and the needle is up against the stop. The force of the slipstream past the controls is holding the stick rigid. With the full strength of both arms I can't move it so much as one millimetre.

Still 3,000 metres to the ground!

I press the knob of the trimmer cautiously towards

"tail-heavy." I only dare switch on the small electric motor which adjusts the control surface for a second at a time, since the strength of the airflow could otherwise easily put it out of action.

The engine cowling starts to rise in front of me— higher still—then moves above the horizon. In a few seconds my machine climbs once more for over a thousand metres. The tremendous pressure of the pull-out on my body has deprived me of all strength to move the controls, it's as if a hundredweight were bearing down on me. The sky is flecked with red—at least that's how my eyes see it. My head is cold and my fingers stiff and rigid.

But a few seconds only passed before the veil was torn from before me, and my aircraft once again responded to me.

As I flew towards home, I met seven parachutes on the way—they might easily be from my first bomber. They hung in the sky like a Jacob's ladder, the steps in the order in which the men had jumped. Only the last of them had broken the series and formed a higher step. He must have been smaller and lighter than the others and for this reason be falling more slowly towards the ground. As I flew up to have a look at my victim I saw that there was only half a body hanging in the straps of the last parachute: the legs and the lower part seemed to have been torn off, probably by a burst of fire from either friend or foe, for the American might well have drifted across a line of fire. The insides were dangling in protruding, bloody tatters from the severed upper half.

A machine which had been badly hit landed just behind me. When we examined it we found thirty-eight hits. On the under side of the wing was smeared a grey substance with bloodstains all around: a man's brains. The pilot reported he had collided with a parachute in the heat of the fight and that the poor devil suspended beneath it must have been hurled by the fearful impact against the metal surface of the wing.

One by one, single aircraft were still sweeping in to land: all that was left of our proud sixty.

We thought one or two had probably landed on other airfields in Holland or Belgium, and our hopes rose, hour by hour, as the German telephone network was operating excellently. Ulrich and Werner came in late, too, and it was only finally at midnight that we could empty our glasses of champagne in honour of the living and the dead. Out of sixty, more than thirty of our comrades had fallen. Many more fought on against their sufferings in hospital, and among them was a cadet-pilot called George.

CHAPTER VIII

THE casualties had never before been so heavy. The remnants of the squadron sat down depressed to breakfast, and answered the greeting of the new Staffelkapitän with a lazy "G'morning."

"Hinterschallers!" called Papi, our guide, philosopher and friend. The mess-sergeant hurried up in his servile way to find out what the Kapitän required.

"Is your name Hinterschallers?"

"No, Herr Hauptmann, it isn't, only people will insist on calling me by that name."

The Chief shook his head with deliberation.

"Well, Hinterschallers, kindly bring me some ration bread. I can't look at this puppy-meal any longer. Nothing but white bread, day after day!"

The fat mess-sergeant shrugged his shoulders regretfully. "Unfortunately we only get white bread for the Herren Flugzeugführer. Ration bread, Herr Hauptmann, brings on flatulence, which is not good for airmen."

We grinned; this was always Hinterschallers's way. The Kapitän looked up in astonishment.

"Flatulence bad for airmen!" he repeated incredulously, raising his voice. "Who ever heard of such a thing! Do you always express yourself in such language?"

"Certainly, Herr Hauptmann, and from the professional standpoint I am particularly anxious that what I say should be taken seriously. Still, apart from that, flatulence really can sour one's life."

We roared with laughter. Only Hinterschallers was still serious, and now assumed a declamatory attitude.

"Take Hinterschallers's Ex-tablets——" and we all joined in the chorus "—*and your wind will ne'er go free— involuntarily!*"

And here, as he always did on such occasions, Hinterschallers proudly drew out his wallet, so as finally to win over the speechless Kapitän. Showy photographs and testimonials from the blessed years of peace advertised the firm of Hinterschaller o.H.G.'s Laboratory for digestive preparations, whose most successful general representative our very own Hinterschallers had once been.

"Get up, *meine Herren*!" the Kapitän finally called. "Otherwise we'll be late at the airfield!"

"Permit me most respectfully," threw in Hinterschallers with a deep bow, "to get the baggage of the Herren ready in the meantime."

"What sort of baggage?" we shouted expectantly, hoping for another joke. Slyly, but with the self-confident air of the influential and knowledgeable he replied,

"Isn't the squadron off to the south of France for a rest, to Perpignan by the Mediterranean, *meine Herren*, to the foot of the Pyrenees, down south where the palms . . . ?"

"Where did you get that from?" the Kapitän interrupted, and Hinterschallers began an affected description of how the Mess Orderlies' grape-vine in all—even the most select—headquarters functioned far better than official information channels. . . .

Finally the Chief rang up the Kommandeur to confirm.

"Yes," he was told. "The order has just come through. Get ready to move!"

77

CHAPTER IX

AN occasional fresh breeze was our only respite from the burning heat of the south. We could almost touch the great mass of the Pyrenees behind us, while in front the deep blue of the Mediterranean stretched away, unlimited by any horizon—utterly merged with the blue of the sky. Before us lay the town, built of a whitish-yellow stone exactly the colour of the sand on the beach, the shape of its houses a reminder of the Moorish invasion.

The landscape and every living thing upon it lay suffering dumbly beneath the burning sun, scarcely daring to breathe. In front of the city gates, between the hovels occupied by Red-Spanish refugees, children and dogs squatted in the shade of slender poplars or ruined huts. Sauntering to the hotel in our Luftwaffe flying-boots, Hitler Youth shorts, R.A.F. bush shirts and Afrika Korps sun-helmets, we were at last able to draw breath in the cool glass-roofed interior of our quarters.

"*Achtung!*" cried Ulrich, refreshed. "Now we get going!"

Twisting his features into that expression of outward amiability which is normally characteristic of the French, he addressed himself without embarrassment to a young blonde drinking lemonade at one of the tables.

"*Pardon, mademoiselle, est-ce que mademoiselle a déjà disposé de son soir?*"

78

The French girl looked up for a moment, laid down her straw and replied, with a charming smile,

"*Non, monsieur, mademoiselle ne l'a pas.*"

She then applied herself once more to her lemonade, as though not a word had passed between them.

Ulrich hesitated—struggling with the French vocabulary. Werner and I moved off—the game was too ridiculous. But soon afterwards Ulrich turned up in our apartment, his eyes shining, but contempt at the corners of his mouth.

"You cowards!"—and then more normally: "Her name's Simone. Big dinner-party this evening. I shall expect the cowards in the foyer at eight o'clock. Evening dress—white shirts!"

"Please don't always call me mademoiselle, call me madame!" Simone said. Madame was twenty-four years old and a picture of unusual loveliness. Her husband had been a civil pilot before he was killed in a storm over the Pyrenees. The young widow came from the best of families and was now studying medicine. As the three of us pooled our vocabulary to sustain the conversation, she made light of our efforts.

"Speak German. I am quite happy speaking and listening to it myself."

We laughed, and she with us, though she didn't know just why. Simone gave a commentary on every dish that was served. We went from onions to Hitler, from Hitler to the war, and from the war to our prospects for the future.

"I like Germans," she observed, "but Germany is going to be beaten."

We stopped eating and looked at her with astonishment.

"The English and Americans will soon be landing in our France—so they say."

We smiled at this naïveté.

"Have you ever heard anything of a certain Atlantic Wall?" Werner asked, without expecting a reply.

"Yes, it's some fortifications made up of a few guns, rather more cement and a good deal more imagination."

Werner was offended. "Where do you get that from? You've not yet seen the Atlantic Wall."

"Well, that's what they say about it. Have you seen it?"

That was a difficult one, as we too had never been face to face with it, even though we frequently flew hundreds of kilometres along the coast. Werner bit his lip.

"Oh, let's forget it!" She raised her glass. "Here's to the end of the war and to having peace once again."

"Amen!" Ulrich echoed.

Where shall we go to now? was the next question. Ulrich suggested *"Budenzauber"* in our rooms.

"Come and have tea with me at home," Simone suggested. We couldn't resist an invitation like that, and so followed her off to where she lived.

As, with some curiosity, we approached the small villa on the edge of the town Madame paused.

"When you get inside, you must promise to send me a nice, large picture for my gallery."

We looked at each other helplessly, not having reckoned on such an unfair request.

"Come in."

We entered a broad, tastefully decorated living-room, on the walls of which hung a good two dozen pictures of airmen—photographs neatly framed and mounted beside one another.

"Ask any of those whom I have hung up there about Perpignan, and they'll tell you about Simone."

It certainly was a curiosity. Below the upper row of

80

portraits of British and French airmen hung the pictures of well-known German pilots, with the Ritterkreuz just below the Victoria Cross. But in the bottom row there were only empty frames.

"Oh, I'm going to fill those up too. They'll be full of English and Americans, who will soon be here to set our France free."

There was an uncomfortable silence. "Nevertheless I love you all," she went on, "French, English, American and German airmen, and I have often cried, because you have to kill one another, whenever any of them has been reported as dead."

All at once Simone had become a riddle to us. Why should this lovely young woman be so dependent on these men over whom she so often wept?

She read our thoughts while we were still standing there by the portraits.

"He loved flying much more than he loved me. But he crashed. That's why for his sake I love flying and all men who love it as much as he did."

We sat down in our armchairs without speaking, with a feeling of the greatest respect for such a person as Simone. She had quite won our hearts.

"Oh, let's talk of something else, it's all too sad! Come on, we're now going to enjoy ourselves!"

Her door was flung open.

"*Bon, c'est Danielle—mon amie.* Her mother was German. Danielle always keeps my house full of people. She's the greatest fun."

We had risen politely to our feet, automatically cheered up as a vivacious, dark-haired girl burst into the room. Simone introduced us.

"Danielle isn't awfully fond of flying. I think she prefers the airmen themselves." And, turning to her friend, "No politics, please, Danielle! Whereas I shall go and get the teas."

The nineteen-year-old made a face.

"You talk like my great-grandmother: 'Whereas I shall go and get the teas'—pouf!"

Simone went off and we had some music. Danielle laughed and sang. Her personality and the naïve unaffectedness of her manner made her most attractive. Simone soon returned, bringing "the teas." We danced and laughed too. Life was good. . . .

Suddenly Danielle jumped to the radio: the B.B.C. news was coming over the air. As if absorbed in her devotions, she knelt before the loud-speaker as the short drum-beats with the final deeper note rang out uncannily through the room.

Kneeling, she had clenched her fists and, though we couldn't see her face, seemed to be trembling. Her slim body was bent forward tensely and the long dark hair had slipped forward from her shoulders. We scarcely dared to breathe, for the girl's attitude had gripped us too.

Now Danielle started to whisper something, and as the drum-beats sounded again, her voice rose.

"*Sauvez la France!*"

We were waiting for the next drum-beat from the radio when Danielle suddenly turned her face towards us, her eyes full of hate and her mouth distorted.

"Go away!" she exclaimed, in a hoarse whisper. "Get out of our country!"

Werner and I had jumped to our feet—we hadn't expected this. Simone was standing before her friend with tears in her eyes, imploring her to be silent. The B.B.C.'s identification signal had ceased, and the news was now being read.

Simone looked at us helplessly: "Forgive her—she's not herself!"

"No!" the other screamed, her eyes flashing. "No, get out! All France hates you!"

And she dropped sobbing into an armchair, shuddering uncontrollably.

We stood as if rooted to the spot. "Stupid girl," Ulrich murmured into the silence.

Werner and I left the room quickly, without saying goodbye.

"I'm staying," Ulrich called, half amused, half touched. "I want to convert her."

Simone came out after us. "Forgive her and forget it! She's sick with hysteria. Forget it, please! She won't ever be here again when you are about!"

How downcast we were as we stepped out into the cool of the night, with Simone standing motionless in the doorway behind us. Only her outline and her shadow were visible, but we knew she was crying. We shook her hand.

"We shall be coming again, Madame."

Werner and I walked homewards, leaving Ulrich with Danielle.

CHAPTER X

"GET up, turn out!—Invasion, turn out, get up!"
At such moments I loathed Hinterschallers,
and would willingly have ordered him out himself.
But he would take no excuse when it was a case of calling
in the morning. I turned over sleepily on to the other
side, but Hinterschallers was inflexible.

"Get up, turn out—invasion!"

He pulled off my blanket—a thing he had never done
before.

"You're off your head!"

"Invasion!" he roared back in the same tone and
rushed into the next room, where I heard the same word
repeated.

"What's up?"

"They've landed in Normandy!"

An hour later we were sitting in our aircraft—Ulrich
still in his best uniform, which he hadn't had time to
change since the evening before. A heavy long-range tank
hung like a bomb beneath each fuselage. Once more the
white town slipped away from beneath us. It was like
looking at a picture-book. We could peer down, but only
for seconds at a time, between fuselage and wing, for our
machines were separated only by a few metres from one
another. Once already two aircraft had collided over
Perpignan, and had fallen right into the hospital cook-
house.

Perpignan seemed to us like a fairy town, probably

because we were not to return to it. City and countryside alike lay wrapped in faery—the dark-eyed, dark-haired girls below, the dirty cottages and cheap cafés, the dust of the streets, palms, pines and vineyards, the blue of sky and sea and the sandy shore.

In a wide sweep we half grazed the Pyrenees, almost close enough to touch their first slopes. A small monastery stood quivering, tottering on its rock—the monks must have needed hours to travel down into the valley, compared with the seconds it took us.

The gates to Spain disappeared astern, the clouds around us sliding across them, suspended between the passes over customs guards, smugglers and refugees alike.

We climbed high up into these peaceful woolly masses —guardian angels when the enemy's sitting on your tail and you can hide yourself in them, great petals springing from the ether, heavenly thousand-bloomed hydrangeas.

On them aircraft are cradled as on soft down. The airman who plays with them, sits on them, scratches the bald patches and pops in and out from side to side is a happy man, and—when they draw their skirts aside to let him again see the earth below—an ever freshly astonished one.

Clouds are airmen from the moment of their birth. But while birds, insects and men have all had to learn to fly, to adapt their powers to this end, clouds are the very essence of flight. They rise up like a spirit, a will which scorns all vulgar obstacles, which secretly forsakes the prosaic earth and then towers suddenly high above it, then moves lightly or dejectedly, dancing or storming along.

Now the clouds were making us happy again, helping us to forget that we were, after all, simply flying projectiles, human rockets. Our aircraft flew widely separated, the white walls, through which we drove unharmed,

85

rising sheer above us. In that milky vapour motion had apparently ceased—the cockpit made up the whole of one's world, its small dimensions the extent of all substance. Time became eternity, until suddenly there was the sun again, throwing our shadows on to the cloud bank below, itself crowned by a rainbow halo.

So our journey across the French countryside drew to its leisurely end. Children of the sky until such time as Mother Earth should call us, now we flew low once again over rivers and forests, towns and villages. Our destination lay somewhere south of Paris, and no one but the Kapitän knew which airfield it was.

As the Eiffel Tower thrust itself needle-like out of the mist over the French capital, we climbed higher and then, with the squadron-leader ahead, dived with increased speed.

"We land here," he called through to us as we flew low across the dry earth of an airfield.

"Still much too far from Paris," grumbled one of the night-birds. But we landed all the same.

The shining hulls of American bombers were drawing across the sky above us.

"Where's our Sprit, Herr Major?" called the Kapitän from his cockpit as the Airfield Commander approached. This elderly officer could scarcely have seen a single aircraft land on his field in the whole war. Now he pointed significantly at the bombers.

"*There's* Sprit," he said.

"We've got to have Sprit, Herr Major, *Sprit*—I repeat—otherwise we give up!" The Chief jumped angrily from his machine.

"I have orders to fly operational sorties against the invasion from your airfield. Your field has eighty thousand litres of petrol in its tanks for this purpose. My aircraft must be tanked up within an hour. We are armed for the sortie, and Le Bourget is sending ammunition for subsequent operations."

"Yes, I have eighty thousand litres of A3 here. You can have that."

"What! A3? Eighty thousand litres of A3? That's crazy! You can drive your car with A3, Herr Major, but our aircraft won't get off the ground with it."

We stood round in dismay, thirsty men standing before a pool of poisoned water.

So we didn't fly on.

For days we stayed there without petrol, and for days we waited for our essential baggage from Perpignan. At last, when the Allies had already secured their foothold, we were able to take off. Our job was to keep the heavy aircraft away from the invasion front, where our infantry were being swamped by load after load of bombs.

Seven-hundredweight long-range tanks hung beneath our machines; the distance being so great, we had to use them. Soon we had passed Paris on our right and soon, too, the last forts west of Versailles had dropped astern.

We looked ahead. Only half an hour still separated us airmen from the front, from that unreal battlefield on the ground. A small stream, a town to the right, a railway, delicate as a toy—and then a shining surface began to show ahead: where the Seine runs into the sea, the Channel had driven a bay deep inland.

"Four-engined bombers overhead," someone reported. We looked upwards. But the Kapitän held on his course.

"Twenty four-engined bombers to the right," said someone else. But still we flew straight ahead.

"Marauders ahead and above us."

The shape of a two-engined bomber passed directly above us and away—her bomb-bays open. Single fighters were circling around as escort.

"Keep calm!" called the squadron-leader. "They are doing nothing to us." We could easily have let ourselves in for something to no purpose—our job was to relieve the pressure on our army comrades.

Caen already lay five, ten or fifteen minutes behind us —we couldn't reckon how long. We had climbed to five thousand metres, and the sea was glistening on all sides.

"There—right ahead—quite far away!"

Our eyes searched along the coast. Yes, there they were: countless thick dots and strokes, smaller dots and diamonds—the invasion fleet! Black smoke extended in thick woolly masses over the coastal belt. The first bombers should soon be coming for us.

"*Achtung*, Thunderbolts from above!"

About twenty American fighters were circling in a defensive ring scarcely five hundred metres higher than we were. They had painted their engine cowls yellow like ours—all really self-respecting people seemed to do the same. The enemy had spoken with respect about us for years past as the "Yellow noses," and all of a sudden here were newcomers from the U.S.A. trying to put the wind up us with our own fighting colour!

"They'll go for us."

"No they won't," the Kapitän came back, "it's a defensive circle!"

Now we too were flying our "roundabout," circling in the opposite direction from that of the enemy. If nothing happened, this could go on for hours. Time would show who could hold out longest. The enemy would have to break off—we were only waiting for him to dive away. But he made no move to do so.

"Below us—four-engined bombers!"

The Chief now found himself in a quandary. If he attacked the bombers, the American Thunderbolts would at once dive on us—but if he didn't attack, we should not be able to carry out our task.

So we went for the bombers.

"Drop long-range tanks!"

In front of us the wide-shouldered Boeings were growing wider. But we kept looking behind, for enemy fighters coming after us.

They came very quickly, quicker than we had thought possible.

"L Dv 217 part D," roared Ulrich. "On the approach of the enemy, his hostile intent is to be considered prob——" He got no further, for the first smoke-trails from the cannon were flicking past. At the same moment the bombers were looming large in our sights. We kept firing, but the others' guns stopped—you don't fire on your own bombers.

One—two seconds, and we were through.

"Pull up—turn right!" ordered the Kapitän.

I pulled the stick back with both hands and snatched the machine away. The blood was forced down into my legs and my backbone cramped into a bow by the tremendous force of the pull-out. To avoid a blackout I bent my head between my knees. That's what each of us was certainly doing, hoping fervently at the same time he would not be rammed. The engine cowlings rose high above the horizon. In front and above me my comrades were hanging in the air on their propellers while behind me there was no one.

Far away, the bomber-formation was flying on— unharmed.

"We'll attack again!"

Our good new Kapitän was an optimist—he had come from the Eastern Front. But here in the west you could not shoot aircraft down "by numbers." Still, he set off obstinately after them. These bombers must be dealt with!

Our old friends the twenty Thunderbolts were again describing their defensive circles above us.

"*Achtung!* Spitfires from behind and above," several of us shouted all at once, and our heads jerked round. At least three squadrons were diving on us with tremendous speed. There was no sense in turning, for the weight of numbers was too heavy against us, and apart from that the American fighters above were lying in wait like vultures.

"Fly straight on!" the squadron-leader ordered quietly. Six or seven hundred metres still lay between us and the British. "I'll count up to three, then we'll turn on the opposite course!—One, two . . ."

"It's madness, Herr Hauptmann!" called Vogel. "Madness!" repeated Meyer II. At the word "three" the English cannon were already flaming.

We put our noses right down and split up at headlong speed. One by one our aircraft made their escape, flying away low in the direction of Paris.

CHAPTER XI

THIS week and those which followed may have sealed the fate of Germany. The enemy had finally gained a foothold, whilst the unchecked stream of German troops to the rear had created confusion. Someone in the first line of trenches must have started to run. He had taken a second with him, and others followed, news of their panic flight spreading from mouth to mouth. One company had fled, and battalions, regiments and corps had become involved, until finally the whole front had collapsed. Some of them may have retreated to re-form later—in both cases obeying orders; others might think of the families whose breadwinners and protectors they were, and decide they had a right to live; while a third group must have recognized the madness of resistance in face of such enemy superiority—or their nerves refused to do their duty—or they just didn't want to fight any more, all sense of purpose in the struggle lost.

Two generals visited us in the heat of those days: the liaison officer between Hitler and the Luftwaffe in the west, and our own Fighter General. We were fallen in in flying kit to greet the visitor when our own Fighter General appeared, as always, a fat cigar stuck out above his small beard.

"Well, chaps, what am I going to say to you? You can see yourselves how things are. It's pretty bloody."

The second general, who spoke a few minutes later, seemed to be rather less frank. He had just come from the Führer's Headquarters.

We moved away afterwards into a tent, where a heated discussion at once began. The depression of the Head-quarters general was only too easy to understand. He had to keep Hitler informed of the daily state of service-able aircraft, had himself to meet every criticism, and defer patiently and continuously to the complaints and abuse of his Commander-in-Chief. Hitler—so he said—was always working himself up over the fact that on numerous occasions scarcely half of the aircraft reported as serviceable actually took off against the enemy. He had made the effort to come here, to his front-line com-rades, so as to go thoroughly into these false allegations. After a good deal of talk our Kapitän was at last called on to speak.

"Our aircraft are old and tired out," he began. "Maintenance services are insufficient, and both material and workmanship faulty. Petrol and ammunition are lying about on the railways, where they've been bombed, and never get here. The training of our young pilots is inadequate, most of them getting shot down during their first sorties. Bombers and low-flying aircraft are ruining our airfields—after every shower the dispersal areas are under water. The order to take off frequently arrives either when the enemy is right over the airfield or has already passed on. And so," the Kapitän ended his lament, "when an emergency take-off finally does make an interception, the enemy superiority is too great."

The generals looked at one another. The younger of them, himself one of our best fighter-pilots, nodded in agreement. But the other shook his head, apparently unable to accept it all.

"Yes, *meine Herren*, I know your difficulties. They are mine too. But I can't tell the Führer that. He simply won't listen to this kind of thing, do you understand? He won't have facts like these reported to him, because they make the situation too obvious. He just doesn't want to have them clearly explained to him. The Führer wants to know how things can be improved, if you follow me, not to hear why they have become so bad."

His tone of voice had become hard and bitter. He walked to his car with his head bowed. He had a long journey ahead of him, past the disorderly columns streaming back in flight towards the German frontier and final defeat. And all that he had seen and heard his supreme warlord would not accept.

Werner and I too felt, a few days after the visit of the two generals, that we had to have a look at the spectacle of the retreating troops. We had a few hours "leave" in which to visit George in his hospital in Northern France. When the first word had come back from there that George was blind and so disfigured that one could scarcely bear to look at him, we had written him off from our squadron: a blind man couldn't fly any more, and a burned face would have been a constant, unnerving reminder of the possibility of our suffering a similar fate.

But now we were acting in response to an invitation from the head of the hospital, who had asked for two of George's squadron-mates, two whom he knew well, to come along. It had to do with an experiment which might be of decisive importance for the wounded man.

So here we were sailing slowly northward in our Storch. The weather was misty, and we need fear no enemy attack. Werner, sitting in front, held the stick, and I the map, and both of us kept our eyes on the high road below. Now and again I tapped my companion on the shoulder when we had taken a "wrong turning." Then we would circle above a cross-roads, fly up to the nameboard of the next railway station or land in a field beside the trees flanking the main road to smoke a cigarette and ask the way from the next passer-by.

We met German troops everywhere—all going north. Finally we turned down our last "side-turning" and in a few minutes reached the small town which was our destination.

The head doctor received us in his room.

"Thank you for coming, *meine Herren*. You know your friend George is blind. Here, as so frequently in wound cases like his, it's a question of nerves. We have some justification for hoping that the cadet is learning to see again. The physical conditions are satisfactory. But the young nursing sister, Celestine, who sits by his bed is possessed of unusual hypnotic powers. She has already made a considerable contribution towards a cure, and is now going to start the experiment in your presence. So, *meine Herren*, we can get going. You yourselves will only be 'supers' in the cast, but please be as pleasant and as cheerful as possible in greeting your friend."

A horrible stench of ether met us as we entered the sick-room. I hardly dared to breathe. George lay in front of us in bed—a swathed bundle. Only the tip of his nose and two staring eyes peeped from the bandages. I could have howled when I looked at the poor devil. But I pulled myself together somehow.

"Hullo, George, old fellow! We thought we would call in and pass the time of day."

"Well, I'm blowed. It's you. Knew you by your voice. Who else is with you?"

"The head doctor and another from the squadron whom you know well."

"Who?"

"I give you three guesses!"

"Ulrich?"

"No."

"Well, come along, tell me who it is. After all, I can't see!"

"But, George," interrupted the dark-haired sister, signing to us to keep quiet, "you can see if only you wish to do so. Now act as though you were looking at the two of them. Wish hard that you can see them. But you must really concentrate hard on this wish. Imagine the face of your friend in front of you, and then see him!"

At this the sister grasped his hands and raised him up in bed.

"Yes, Celestine," answered George, as though speaking in his sleep, "I am wishing. . . ."

His eyes stared at me, and I forced myself to meet his dead gaze. I could hear my own breathing, all had become so quiet and strained. Once I had stood guard by the coffin of a dead comrade, but this present moment seemed even more endless: the empty look of the man opposite me was not going to come alive. My knees shook. Those eyes were unbearable. The sister's black hair was a dark spot in the corner of my field of vision, and I wanted to look at her hair, but George's eyes were still staring at me, and I had got to stick it out. What should I say if he recognized me? And—far worse—what should I say if the experiment failed?

"Now you *can* see!" exclaimed the sister.

It was then I noticed how my friend's pupils were contracting, the corners of his eyes wrinkling. His gaze moved slowly away from mine, then shifted quickly back.

"I can see you," George said softly. "Werner is standing beside you. . . ."

We dared not stir. George had laid himself back on his pillow.

"I can see—see—see," he murmured again and again, keeping his eyes shut. Suddenly he sat straight up in bed.

"Man!—I can see again!"

His eyes darted feverishly from one to the other; and as they reached Celestine they paused.

George crumpled up into his blankets and wept.

Werner with his English prisoner.

Before and after the order to take off.

'Struggle as the firemen might, they couldn't get the blaze under control.'

Two Spitfires which fell victim to the 'Abbeville Boys': above, a Mk V of No. 222 Squadron, and, below, a Mk V of No. 412 (Falcon) Squadron, RCAF.

Reichsmarschall Herman Göring makes a tour of inspection.

A group of the 'Abbeville Boys'.

A pilot examines the damaged tail of his aircraft.

Werner wearing his oxygen mask.

Mechanics stand by while the author prepares to take off.

Airborne.

Field-Marshal Irwin Rommel inspects a fighter station near the English Channel.

Hitler eats Christmas dinner with Adolf Galland and fellow pilots in Northern France.

CHAPTER XII

THE Allies were advancing faster and faster, the front moving ceaselessly closer. At times when the wind was blowing from the west we could hear its thunder.

Our sorties became more difficult and took a heavier toll every day. We nearly always flew home with a shot in the fuselage, a hole in the wing or a damaged engine.

Now I had a new engine to "fly in." There was no enemy in the air for miles around. I sat hunched in my cockpit, examining the jumble of knobs, buttons, levers and dials. For some reason I was not in a good frame of mind—fear perhaps.

The aircraft exhaled its special smell beneath the blazing sun, and I could almost taste the hot breath of its machinery—that mixture of metal, rubber, petrol and oil that was something like the smell of a "Maggi" bottle. But I loved this aroma, this exhalation, as a horseman loves the smell of his mount's sweat. I set the altimeter to zero, checked the oxygen supply and illuminated the sights. And then my arms dropped limply between my knees.

I thought of all the things that could go wrong: there were thousands of possibilities of failure, but only one of two alternative consequences to all of them—either life or death. But Death had other opportunities than these. He gathered his own to himself without having to crook a finger. We did his work for him, and the others did it

97

for him too. He had no need to wait for one of these technical failures or for an airman to make a mistake. Perhaps he was already sitting beside me, or in an enemy's cockpit and aiming at me! And where did God come in?

I laughed aloud. Perhaps dear God above was concerned simply that we should prove ourselves—each one of us in his own problem and in that situation to which life had called him. Well, that meant me, and so—start up!

As I started the engine, the sudden roar gave me a shock. The power behind that tremendous din made me shudder.

With clenched teeth I pressed the throttle-lever forward. The great engine snatched me across the grass with the impetuous force of a wild stallion. The earth glided away beneath me. I was flying—and everything was all right once more. I laughed at my weakness. The aircraft responded to the gentlest touch on the controls—yes, aircraft in the air were always gentle!

In my high spirits I started to sing—loudly.

"Look out! The Tommies are careful listeners," Werner warned me over the radio—he must have heard my singing from the ground station.

"*Achtung! Three Spitfires airborne!*"

I pulled myself together, and in the same instant saw the enemy flight approaching me—it was too late to run for it, and I couldn't land, for they would certainly have shot me up on the ground. I had to accept the unequal fight.

The illuminated sight glowed in front of me, and within it three small horizontal marks, with a point in the middle of each which was a human being who wanted to shoot me—all three of them wanted to shoot me down!

98

The marks grew visibly in size and began to show up their outline of wings, fuselage and engines.

I was looking down the gun-muzzles of the left-hand pilot. Three sets of six cannon flashed out at me—and my own hands pressed hard on the firing-levers. Four hearts stopped for a moment as the fire spurted from the guns into their faces, four heads ducked down at the same instant, as each thought he was going to ram the enemy—each himself a projectile—but too late to alter the outcome, too late even for a last thought. I burst through the enemy formation like the crack of a whip, grazing them by a hair's-breadth and pulling my aircraft up vertically, the breath pressed out of my body and the blood hammering in the arteries of my neck. I had no idea whether I had been hit.

"Hold on! Vogel and Meyer II are taking off," I heard in my earphones. Werner had seen it all coming.

Beneath me lay the airfield, and two aircraft were rising from it—Vogel and Meyer II—the two who fought like ten. It wasn't often that such a take-off succeeded, since both pilot and aircraft were preoccupied with getting off the ground, and the enemy would wait above them like a hawk and swoop on to them while they were still defenceless.

Two Britons had already dived down, but my comrades were flying calmly straight ahead. Then they hauled their aircraft abruptly round. Their guns flashed briefly— Vogel and Meyer II usually only needed one burst to win.

The third Tommy was mine. I had almost forgotten him; and as my head swivelled his first shells whipped towards me. I turned sharply inside, for the Briton, too, was fighting for his life.

99

The turns grew ever tighter and the track upwards ever steeper. Blinding sweat was running into my eyes, forcing tears from them. But I dared not take my eyes from the enemy pursuing me so relentlessly. The engine was giving of its best. My thoughts flew to the fight which Werner had won for me, so like this one. But this time I was alone and would have to win on my own.

My arms were weakening from continually pulling the stick towards me. I had now only one desire to bring my guns to bear from astern of the enemy—each of us struggling for the other's life, and for his own. I could look right into the Spitfire's cockpit, and there I saw him, the Oxford undergraduate or office worker, or whoever he might be. Why had we to shoot one another? Why couldn't we land and shake hands and have a round of skat? Pah! I had become weak as a jelly with this one thought, and now I should have to suffer for it. The damned Tommy had caught up and was sitting close on my tail—one more circle and he'd have me cold!

In desperation I pulled my aircraft up vertically, the other hanging on to me like a burr. But then my slip-stream thrust him backwards along the steep angle of his climb, and he spun away downwards.

I shut my eyes and let the stick go, simply to relax, do nothing, stop thinking—just for a moment. Then I started to shiver. My sweat was cold, and the shivering increased. An icy fit of trembling swept over me—my nerves were failing in their duty. . . .

I opened my eyes wearily, my hands grasping the stick automatically, and the aircraft pulled peacefully out of its dive into the normal flying position.

Far astern I could see my Englishman on his way home. He had become a stranger to me, an unknown passer-by who meant nothing to me. Now I wanted simply to relax, to fly straight and level, using neither will nor intellect, straight on. . . .

Something rattled and scratched in my earphones. Someone was calling up repeatedly, but to me it was just incomprehensible noise. Minutes must have passed, the calls continuing uninterruptedly—till at last I realized it was me that they were calling.

I looked down. Where was I?

The silver ribbon of a stream ran through fields and woods. Reddish-golden strings of pearls flung up towards me, a magnificent show of fireworks, exploding noiselessly in every direction into little smoke-clouds which hovered silently in the air.

But suddenly the roar of the two-thousand horsepower in front of me ceased—the heavy propeller-blades turned slowly once or twice more like the sails of a windmill, and came to rest. The air-stream whistled ominously between them towards me, and now the peaceful-looking golden pearls flying up at me were detonating with loud reports.

All at once I sobered up. It was plain I was being shot at by Flaks. Infantrymen were fighting in trenches and bunkers down below and above them there sailed a passive target, a man in a dream.

My aircraft was dropping frighteningly fast. I hurriedly turned on to the opposite course so as to be able to reach the foremost German positions. The earth slid up towards me and no one was shooting any longer. It was quiet, save for the whistling of the air as it rushed past. Banks, roads and bushes grew larger and larger, drawing away ever faster beneath me.

The first stones struck the underside of my aircraft as it ploughed a long furrow in the earth like a heavy skate and with a final groan came at last to rest.

As I unstrapped myself with weary hands, Vogel and Meyer II roared close over my head. They had followed me, but now they couldn't help me any more.

The dynamo which fed my radio-transmitter only worked when the engine was running, so I switched on the battery. As my two comrades flew again and again over my aircraft I heard their message.

"Stay by the aircraft! We'll come and pick you up."

"We'll come and pick you up." That didn't sound like our side of the lines, or the enemy's. What could it mean? Nobody needed to pick me up from our own side. And if this was an enemy-occupied area I should be a prisoner in a few minutes.

The sun blazed relentlessly down. I was hungry and thirsty, and my last cigarette had been smoked. There was firing away to the west, and gunfire could be heard from south, north and east as well. It must be no-man's land here.

The warm air shimmering above the fields gave an impression of great peace, and in the short intervals between the firing I listened to a lark trilling somewhere nearby. But then the muffled thunder rolled up once more through the midday air.

I had hidden myself in a patch of broom close by whose branches might hide me from the low-flying enemy hunting continuously for their prey. My friends won't be able to fetch me by daylight, I thought—for our rescue aircraft was a slow-flying Storch which had neither weapons nor armour. I couldn't possibly start searching for German troops, but just had to wait where I was if I wanted to be picked up.

From time to time I ran to my machine, switched on the battery and spoke to the ground station at our airfield.

"I'll come at midnight when the moon's up," Werner

explained. But by that time clouds might have gathered and make landing impossible in the darkness—besides, the advancing front might get here first. Oh, the success of a rescue depended on so many different things.

The afternoon went by terribly slowly, with the din of the front moving up closer from all sides. When I pressed my ear to the ground I could catch the throbbing of heavy engines and the clank of armoured tracks.

This place was eerie, all living creatures seeming to sense their impending destruction. Hares, birds and insects scenting the unknown peril awaited disaster, trembling in their hides. And men—friend or foe—who in the same distressful way had perhaps dug themselves into this earth somewhere round, were peering fearfully about them now so that they could find and mutilate each other.

"Hands up!"

A rifle barrel was glaring at me. When I saw it was a German infantryman I had to laugh.

"That's my aircraft over there. Surely you know the German Cross?"

He dropped his weapon at once and lay down beside me. He didn't speak a word, his eyes fixed on the crest of the low chain of hills opposite.

"Where are our lines?" I asked.

The other stared in front of him and didn't answer. His manner was obstinate and sullen. The salt from his sweat or his tears had washed clean lanes in the caked dust on his face, the smell of his sweat-soaked uniform mingling with the odour of freshly turned earth. His gaze was still fixed on the hills.

"They'll come when it gets dark!" he murmured, and fumbling in his pocket produced paper and tobacco-dust from which he rolled a cigarette with stiff, clumsy fingers.

"Who'll come?"

My companion looked at me doubtfully as though I was not quite normal.

"The Shermans of course."

I passed him a match.

"H'm, bit of a pansy," he said sarcastically and a little pityingly, indicting my well kept nails. "Here, have a go," he offered, after the first draw at his cigarette. We smoked the rest of it together.

"Where will they attack from?"

"We don't ask 'where from.' They come from everywhere," declared my neighbour. "If you're penned in a corner you only ask 'when,' if you get me—*when* does the drive start, *when*!"

Now at last I understood the significance of this great neutral expanse we were in. Death had already stretched his arm over this ground, simply granted it a respite of a few brief, ominous hours before the assault of the tanks and guns which were to be launched into it from all directions.

"Man, you've no idea what they can do!" the infantryman began once more. "They make mincemeat out of us!" He pointed behind him towards a small plantation. "There are still two hundred men of our regiment over there. When we were trying to surrender during the day we had to cross bare slopes—they shot us to bits there. At night there wasn't any mercy from the devils, either. As soon as it gets dark they attack with heavy tanks and flame-throwers with a range fifty metres wide. Or else they come over with flails against our mines, and great ploughs. If you're lying in the trenches they trample you in and bury you alive."

I wasn't enjoying this description and gave him a nudge.

"Well anyway, I'm going to be picked up at midnight by a Storch."

He looked at me with wide eyes.

"Take me too, man, take me with you!" And he fumbled in his pocket with excitement and produced a tattered photograph. "Here—my little girl, my boy, my wife!"

I looked at the picture of his family, the two children of about school age with the mother between them, in front of their neat, small house. On the back, in a young woman's handwriting was written, "Mother, Peter and Irene pray every day for Daddy, for him to come back to us soon."

Mother, Peter and Irene—I thought—there are millions of such. Over there in the wood other fathers or grown-up Peters were lying dead.

"You *must* take me with you!" the other repeated insistently. "It's for the children, man!"

I nodded. Someone was calling to us from the bushes. A second infantryman had crawled up to us, doubtless to see what had become of his comrade. I was still holding the family picture of the first in my hand as the second lay down beside us with an interrogatory gesture.

"Getting soft, aren't you? Enough of that nonsense. There's only one thing for it now—to kill as many Tommies and Americans as we can before they finish us off. He cleared his throat noisily and spat.

"You can fly with us too," I said, after a little thought. "If you've got a strong belt, we'll lash you to the strut."

The newcomer seemed not to understand. But when I explained what I meant his lips began to quiver—his turn to get soft.

Just before the blazing red ball of the sun dipped in the north-west, Vogel and Meyer II, with Werner, had circled several times above us; the navigation problem which Werner had to solve during the coming night was a very difficult one and it was important to make a check of the landmarks around me. Bright stars were already shining here and there from the dark-grey sky.

Night fell soon afterwards. Now and then I climbed into my aircraft to talk to Werner.

"Come earlier!" I asked him.

But that was impossible, he had to wait for moonlight. Meanwhile the din of battle had started up afresh on every side, the clatter, rolling and pitching of tanks growing louder and clearer.

Thousands of gun-barrels flashed and thundered, tall columns of fire rising into the night sky behind the hillocks. The air seemed literally to boil, and the earth shook. One thought possessed all three of us—the tanks mustn't get here before midnight. . . .

But they came.

The moon had just risen, but something like a massive bank of cloud was approaching from the westward. A little before midnight the tanks rolled forward from the crest of the ridge opposite. Beneath the cold light of the moon they looked like gigantic, hideous toads whose throats spat blazing oil. These were the flame-throwers, which shrivelled everything in their path and before which agonised bodies were crumpled and charred.

We still crouched beside my aircraft, for Werner must by now be on his way. I held the Very pistol in my right hand, ready to give the agreed signal. I also emptied the petrol-tank, as the curtain of gunfire was now only a few hundred paces away, the first shapes hurrying in our direction, and my only weapon the Very pistol. The two infantrymen brought their rifles to the ready. But the next minute we saw German steel helmets—sharpshooters, who must have dug themselves in well in front for a last rearguard action, and now dropped breathlessly to the ground beside us.

"They're coming!"

A lieutenant was lying beside me.

"It's no use," he groaned, "you can't knock out armour with pistols and hand-grenades." When he heard we were expecting a rescue aircraft he looked at me.

"Is it a big one?"

"No. It can only take three at the outside."

He thrust a wallet into my hand.

"Tell them I have been killed"—and without pausing he put the barrel of his revolver to his temple and pulled the trigger. . . .

Gunfire shattered our eardrums, bullets whipped past, and the flame-throwers mewed and spat. Screams rang out and the earth shuddered glaring reddish-yellow muzzle flashes lighting up the night.

As the hands of my watch reached twelve a shadow slipped across the moon. For a few seconds we heard the hum of a descending aircraft.

"You're right above us. Circle!" I called into the radio, then fired the three green lights. With the last Very cartridge I turned my own aircraft into a blazing landmark.

The tanks were rolling forward and searchlights sweeping as the Storch landed right alongside my machine. Before it had stopped we were at it, running. Werner hauled me inside, half a dozen infantrymen crowding behind me.

"Take us with you!"

I wanted to take the man whose picture of his wife and children I could still see before me, but he had been left behind in the crush; others had been stronger. A big man forced himself in on top of me.

"That's enough. We've got to get going!" Werner called.

Suddenly it grew light as day—the beam of a search-light was on us. Werner opened his throttle wide.

Outside, a few were clinging desperately to the struts, among them my two infantrymen of the afternoon.

With this load on it, the Storch couldn't rise from the ground. Werner was roaring with fury. Bullets were smashing into the wings, to left and right the men on the struts being shot to pieces. As it moved away beneath us three bodies slid to the ground. The aircraft rose into the air just in front of a wood. . . .

As we came down a few minutes later in a small valley, safe now from the enemy's fire, I couldn't stop myself thinking of that first man who had dropped back to earth with the others. Perhaps he was lying wounded some-where between the furrows, his hands before his face, waiting for the blazing oil of the flame-throwers to roast him to death, that family photograph crumbling to ashes on which his young wife had written: "Mother, Peter and Irene pray every day for Daddy, for him to come back to us soon."

The night's storm-clouds had gathered meanwhile, great blue-black masses plunging everything into pitch-darkness, except for the lightning flashes whipping every second across the sky. Their leaden masses hung im-mobile above the landscape, unwilling to yield a drop of rain. The thunder—like the rolling of fire from gigantic mortars—lasted well into the morning hours.

We stood in silence and looked back the way we had come. Only a few dozen miles to the west, the battle of extermination was raging . . . the agonised screams of the wounded, the lust to kill, the grin behind the gun-sights, the muzzles spitting death, the souls flitting from the field of slaughter—and now, thunder and lightning over all. In endless procession the lifeless battalions were rising from the ground, uncanny figures rearing into black cloud-shapes. So viewed, perhaps after all the struggle had a meaning, as a conflict of ideals—that was godlike; if of false ideals—that was human. Only the means were diabolical.

CHAPTER XIII

HINTERSCHALLERS had brought the luggage to the car. We were standing round the Kapitän. "We take off at 9.30 in accordance with the orders for the move, the air situation permitting. Please check watches: it's now eight minutes past nine—intermediate landing at Düsseldorf. Fresh instructions there. You"—the Chief turned to me—"proceed to Le Bourget and get yourself a replacement aircraft. Any questions?"

Ulrich raised his arm with a semi-serious expression. "Couldn't we first pay one more visit to Perpignan?" Everybody laughed, the Kapitän included as he shook his head:

"Thank you, *meine Herren*."

Five minutes before take-off Ulrich was called to the telephone. He only came back just as the engines of the squadron were starting up and ran across to me.

"Danielle is in Versailles at the Kommandantur. She wants to see me. She's got to come with me to Germany, do you hear, she's got to come."

"The little girl from Perpignan?"

"Danielle's no little girl, I tell you." He nearly pulled my hand from my arm. "Say after me, 'I promise you to bring Danielle to Germany.' Go on, say it!"

"That's extortion. Is it as serious as all that, then, between you and little—little Danielle?"

"Yes, you idiot," he replied emphatically, looking round anxiously at the others, who were already taking off.

"How serious, then?"

"I want to marry her. Go on now, promise me!"

"All right, Ulrich, I don't yet know, actually, how I can manage it, but I'll do my very best."

Ulrich came close up to me and twiddled the top button of my tunic. His speech was slow and subdued.

"If anything should happen to me, look after her in Germany. You know how I feel about it. *Compris?*"

At that he jumped into his aircraft and roared off after the others. He's to be envied all right, I thought, as I followed him with my eyes and placed Danielle in my imagination by his side.

It was only when the aircraft had vanished into the mist over Paris that it dawned on me what a responsibility I should be taking on myself in carrying out my promise.

By midday the squadron was already well on its way home while on the ground Hinterschallers was still trying to get the car to go. The last mechanics of the rear party were blowing up the hangars, setting the barracks alight and making their getaway as quickly as possible—it was said the leading American tanks were already in the woods close to our airfield.

When at last we were ready to leave the sinister figures of French civilians were already moving about in the bushes. As we passed the fuelling-point, the Kommandant waved. He was sitting on a block of cement and appeared to be waiting.

"Still here, Herr Major?"

The elderly officer, who had certainly not seen the front since 1918, sounded perplexed and anxious.

"What ought I to do—what can I do? I'm sitting on my eighty thousand litres of A3, and I've got to set them alight before the Allies arrive. I shall answer for it with my head—here are the fuse-wires, already in position. I was just going to make the switch, but now at the last moment someone has given me an order to wait for some tanks which want fuel. Really, what *ought* I to do?"

The Major was plucking at his hair. He had lived a peaceful existence in the rear for years past, had never done anyone any harm. He pressed his hands before his face and could well have wept now that, at the threshold of his declining years, for the first time his life was at stake.

"I'm afraid we must get on, Herr Major."

He nodded. "If you see the tanks, show them the way here and tell them they had better hurry."

We drove fast along the highroad to Paris. Great mushrooms of smoke were springing up all round the horizon and black curtains were beginning to cover the sky—blown-up ammunition depots and burning petrol dumps.

Low-flying American aircraft were circling close above the ground, looking for targets, ready any moment to dive to the attack. Electric overhead tram-cables dangled confusedly above the asphalt. Swollen bodies of dead horses and metal frames of destroyed cars already rusting filled the ditches; everywhere there were ashes of burnt-out seats and tyres, a stench of burnt rubber and rotting flesh. From time to time a pack of wild dogs or a black cloud of flies emerged from the source of this sweet, penetrating odour.

Here and there Frenchmen were patrolling in the bushes and woods—the kind of people you would have seen at the time of the French Revolution. But this time they were expecting their friends, the Allies.

At isolated points, in the centre of unprotected fields, hardy gun-crews had dug in their guns to halt the advance of the onward-rolling Shermans. And there, too, were our tanks—a large number of the colossi had found a hiding-place on both sides of the road in a small wood. I stopped, jumped out and went up to the first officer I saw.

"Haven't you any petrol?"

He shook his head dejectedly.

"Over there," I said, pointing towards our distant air-field. "Over there there's an old major sitting on eighty thousand litres, who's anxiously waiting for you."

"Where's that?" asked the other excitedly. I described the way there, but he shook his head. "It's no use. Much too far. We're almost empty."

"We're going back," I called to Hinterschallers, "the major must be told he can blow up his A3."

"It's gone already," Hinterschallers replied. Indeed a gigantic mushroom of black smoke was rising higher and higher into the sky above our airfield.

Low-flying enemy aircraft were still searching along the road. One of them appeared to have seen us, for he circled close above our heads. As Hinterschallers braked sharply we could clearly see the pilot looking down at us. Then he came into the attack.

We jumped into the ditch and looked for the manholes which are situated at intervals of fifty paces along nearly all the *Autobahns*—but just here there seemed only to be isolated ones. I had the good luck to find one at once, but my companion was running up and down like a lunatic when the first bursts flashed down. The shells struck the asphalt beside us and detonated with a frightful din. Hinterschallers had already jumped towards me in desperation and squeezed himself head foremost into the narrow, shallow hole.

We had survived the first attack, but the second would follow in a few seconds, when the pilot would correct his aim, or so we felt convinced.

The attempt to get the two of us into the hole failed: our chests and heads remained unprotected, as it was too narrow for us both to kneel in. I began pulling us both out.

"Quick, get in head first!"

I felt a head was more valuable than two legs, and my companion, who did not at first seem to appreciate my reasoning, quickly followed suit nevertheless as the salvo crashed down. It was a bad moment—I was ready to see his legs shattered. He was gasping away, just as I was, for he had got himself shored up in a pretty awkward position. Fear and standing on one's head are difficult to put up with simultaneously.

The next moment he was jerking convulsively. "I'm hit!" he stammered.

I almost felt glad he was the first, had had to suffer before me. Hoisting myself up I hauled the wounded man from the hole, who had gone the colour of cheese. His trousers had suffered severely but his backside showed only a slight graze.

"I can't stand it any longer!" he burst out. "If he comes at us again I'll shoot him," and he drew his pistol and pushed the safety-catch forward.

The American came in again a few yards above us, flying slowly as if he intended to land. As he circled round us we could clearly see his head and shoulders. Hinterschallers held out his pistol, followed the movement of the aircraft and fired—twice, three times, four times. The American must have seen this, for something amazing happened—he raised his hand to the edge of his helmet.

"He's saluting," I cried, "he's saluting! What a man! You've impressed him with your pistol."

The enemy flew very low past us once more, his propeller almost furrowing the ground—we could practically see his instruments. The pilot was still saluting, still with his hand to his headgear. But then at last we realised he wasn't saluting with his hand, but only with one finger, and that not at his temple, but in the middle of his forehead.

Hinterschallers and I looked at each other in amazement. "That's more than fair," I remarked.

"He's right," Hinterschallers agreed. "We really are idiots. How could one imagine one can shoot down a Thunderbolt with a pistol?"

The American turned away and went in to attack a heavy lorry which was coming up a few hundred yards behind us.

We drove on, the same thought in both our heads—may God be merciful to the others!

At last we reached the suburbs of Paris to find the flood of retreating troops blocking all the roads. Old, patched-up wrecks of cars, double-decker omnibuses from the city transport services, wretchedly armed reservists with captured Czech rifles and ammunition which didn't fit them—it was a sad sight. Our Wehrmacht whose spirit and toughness had once conquered this country was now on the retreat, shuffling along listlessly or maybe with a last spurt of energy as the enemy dictated.

"Stop a moment, Hinterschallers!"

I wanted to discuss Ulrich's plans with the older man in one of the first quiet sidings of the Versailles tramlines.

"We're on our way to the Kommandantur, where there's a girl waiting for us. Her name's Danielle and she wants to come to Germany."

"But not with me!" replied Hinterschallers defensively. "It'll all land on my shoulders—rape, abduction of a French subject and all the rest of it. Can't be done."

"She's Ulrich's fiancée and he wants to marry her in Germany. I've given him my word. . . ."

"That's as may be, and it's a charming situation—very romantic. But as far as I am concerned, *I* haven't given my word."

"All right, let's get on. We'll go there at any rate."

Danielle was sitting on a suitcase in front of the Kommandantur. As we stopped she jumped to her feet, recognizing me. Once again that defiant face from Perpignan—but this Danielle had changed. Her pale face wore the solemn gravity of one about to make a sacrifice. Here was an adult, addressing us in a grown woman's voice. Ulrich was to be envied for having such a girl.

"Oh, thank you!" she cried, flushing, but in whether from shame or unnerved by the prospect of the insecurity before her I couldn't tell.

"Ulrich sends you his love," I managed to say, to get over the distress of the moment somehow.

"Is that all he said?"

"No."

Danielle was waiting, her expression more and more anxious, looking first at me and then at Hinterschallers. She knew quite well we couldn't take her with us. Her forehead wrinkled slightly above her nose, and the eyebrows twitched. I was sorry for her—she looked so hopeless. She began to sob.

"Please, I want to go to Ulrich."

"Take her with you," I begged Hinterschallers, and if I could have persuaded him by falling on my knees I would have done it then.

"No," he said shortly, with all the harshness of which he was capable.

Danielle snatched up her things and hurried away. Hinterschallers hesitated beside me—only one more shock and he would capitulate.

"She's going on to Paris," I said, pityingly. "She'll certainly jump into the Seine when she gets there."

He started and swallowed hard. When he looked at me next, his eyes were staring.

"Will she really do that?"

"Of course, she's that sort of a girl."

We leapt in, and Hinterschallers accelerated hard—a few moments afterwards Danielle was sitting in the car with us. She was still crying, but this time from happiness.

In the confusion of the traffic the population was cheering the steady stream of captured English and Americans being taken back in lorries from the frontline area. The *"Millionenstadt"* of Paris was working no longer. It was on the eve of its greatest day of rejoicing, the day of liberation: France, defeated France, was at last getting back onto its feet.

We had to drive slowly, using side streets, for the active underground movement had strewn their five-pointed nails everywhere. And in fact it happened that one of these, in spite of all precautions, did puncture one of our tyres. The Parisians hung out of their windows in delight at our discomfiture, or indulged their revengeful feelings with a stream of insulting comments as we changed the wheel.

The French pressed continually closer round our car, or, more accurately, they weren't any longer simply standing around, but had deliberately encircled us, as though about to attack at any moment. Their insulting remarks had been succeeded by hostile looks and threatening gestures.

It was only because we had a woman sitting in the car that we were able to avoid the worst. But if Danielle had revealed herself to be a Frenchwoman, she might perhaps have been killed there and then before our eyes. As it was she kept both hands pressed before her face, probably because she believed herself to be playing the hidden rôle of a traitor to her countrymen. It was from this that I realized for the first time how deeply she must have changed, that she could be following a man whom she scarcely knew—following him into a foreign country in the throes of defeat.

I almost grudged Ulrich this girl.

As a precaution, I drew my revolver—after all any one of these lowering Frenchmen might have one in his pocket. As we jumped into the car, an icy silence settled on the jostling mob. Someone gave a scarcely audible order—and the crowd divided before us. They're clearing their line of fire, I thought—when we drive off, they'll shoot. I raised my revolver and covered the nearest bystanders. Luckily that was warning enough for them.

So we hurried on, using our sidelights, to Le Bourget.

A steady stream of old, clumsy transport aircraft with red-cross markings was landing there to pick up the wounded.

"When will you get to Düsseldorf?" I asked, as I passed Danielle and Hinterschallers a Pervitin tablet from my sea-rescue kit, and took one myself to stop going to sleep.

Hinterschallers balanced the tablet on his palm.

"H'm, that'll be enough for twenty-four hours. The rendezvous will be to-morrow afternoon at my house. You have been there once already."

"And how will you get across the frontier?"

"These little chaps'll do the trick," he replied, exhibiting a huge tin of sardines in oil, a bottle of brandy and a packet of cigarettes.

The next moment he was roaring away with Danielle.

I stood for a while looking after the car. What if Ulrich should be killed one day? I was afraid I felt more for Danielle than perhaps I should, but I tried to put such thoughts out of my mind.

CHAPTER XIV

I HAD to fly in darkness—but after the day's events there was nothing very alarming about that. My course was almost north-east and took me over Soissons, Laon, Givet, Lüttich, and north-west past Aachen to Düsseldorf. At best, I was "taking bearings by rule of thumb." For this purpose I took a small map, estimated the course by eye, measured off with a pencil the four hundred kilometres from Paris to Düsseldorf, judged the distances between the towns and rivers over which I was flying, then divided up the total flying-time of sixty minutes and learnt the route by heart in the following fashion:

Take-off. Twelve minutes—small town with river. Twenty minutes—small town with river. Eleven minutes —large town with river. Five minutes—large town on the right. Sixty minutes after take-off—Düsseldorf and the Rhine.

The pilots of the large transports roared with laughter and shook their heads over such methods of navigation. But one oldish Captain nodded his approval.

"That'll get you there all right."

It was already getting dark when I opened up the throttle before the glass windows of the Paris Airport Restaurant, and the wheels of my machine drew away from French soil. France had become a memory—painful only in the leaving of it.

I could still make out the wide highroad along the line

of my course, and the long column of weary men going home. The infantry would need weeks to get them back to Germany. The needle of my air-speed indicator rested motionless at the four-hundred-kilometre mark. In one hour it would drop back to zero, and that would mean that I was home.

The grey veil down below had grown ever thicker over the landscape, but moon and stars gave a good deal of light. In the West, too, night had fallen. The palely gleaming radiance of the luminous dials bothered me, coating my hands and face with a watery green. Beside me the wings shone in the moonlight. I wondered whether some loving couple somewhere on the globe was looking up at the moon and if they saw my shadow. Or perhaps one of the fast Mosquitoes might get me in his sights against the moon's face?

A silvery-blue ribbon was moving towards me, and I recited my piece—"Twelve minutes—small town with river." The Aisne, glittering like a strip of tinsel, had dispersed my anxious thoughts. I looked intently downwards, then to right, left and astern, but no Mosquito was to be seen.

At last I sighted Soissons, and when I turned my head again in the direction I was flying in, there was Laon already in the circle of my propeller.

Now I would have to wait twenty minutes for the next silver streak to appear—an eternity when you have only the monotonous roar of the engine, and land and sky alike seem immobile. Every engine contains something secret within itself, something it doesn't reveal to every pilot. But if the airman has his ear in tune with it, he can lose his gaze in the distance and come to believe the only earthly quality still affecting his senses is the regular, massive droning of his engine. In this way a melody can

be spun out of the innumerable strands of sound, throbbing steadily as from a gigantic organ, weaving in endless
variations, enrapturing the airman and lulling him into
a kind of devoted meditation—till suddenly he jerks into
frightened wakefulness; the monotonous roaring re-
echoes in his ears, and objects loom into reality again.

I began thinking of my own country, whose sons were
now coming home. As prodigals? There would be no
flowers—no cheers for them. Still, people must give them
a word of welcome there: one word would be enough.
Soldiers would need that first word as they trod their
home soil once again, defeated and harried, at the moment
they again set eyes, after years of waiting on the women
and children who spoke and understood their language.

I looked up from my thoughts, in a subconscious
fashion expecting some situation to develop of which I
was not yet aware. Perhaps there was a British night-
fighter behind me? I sideslipped sharply, glanced back
and did a roll in the night sky. And then I just had to
laugh—it was pure fear and nothing else which had got
me by the neck. Meanwhile the luminous paint shimmered on the dials as though from a crawling mass of
thousands of tiny glow-worms, its restless movement
influencing me too, making me feel something *must* be
about to happen. I thought of Danielle and Hinterschallers driving on beneath the same moonlight. They
also had reason to fear the Mosquitoes. I forced myself
to think of the Düsseldorf airfield—there were still forty
more minutes to go. . . .

A shadow had slipped across the moon's disc. I was
sure I had seen it, and as if by its own volition my aircraft
pulled up in a steep turn towards the stars, the pressure of
it thrusting me downwards into my seat. My left hand
switched on the illuminated sight, which lit up so brightly

I had to dim it down. I laid my finger round the trigger guard of my guns—now I was ready. Calmed by this, I turned back again on to my course.

But where had that shadow got to now? I peered round, searching the whole field of the sky, but it wasn't to be seen. A small star was showing low down in the circle of my propeller, but in fact it was too low to be above the horizon. It must be the light from a house or a car, I thought, as apart from it the whole landscape was in darkness. Still, it seemed to come no closer. Could it really be a star? Or was I flying backwards?

My air-speed indicator showed 450 kilometres an hour. I opened the throttle wide, the revolutions quickened, and the needle rose jerkily: 500–550 kilometres. The light still came no closer—and it was veering across more and more to the left. That could only be an aircraft—the same one whose shadow I had seen, perhaps?

I'm no night-fighter, I thought—he'll be more than a match for me. But then it occurred to me that the enemy might be still trying to find a victim, which could be Danielle and Hinterschallers, or anyone else. . . . I turned my machine towards the light and pushed the throttle lever right forward through the gate. The engine could only be run at full power for a minute—its roar rose to a howl—for an aircraft, too, has nerves which can be tortured.

The needle had passed the 650-kilometre mark. The light ahead of me seemed at last to stay where it was, and then—move slowly closer. It must be one of the enemy's fastest types—a Mosquito! The technical data passed through my mind: mid-wing, twin-engined, straight leading-edges between the engines, fixed guns firing astern. . . .

My eyes sketched in the contours round the light. The next moment I sighted the shining cockpit hood and the exhaust flames. Thumb and forefinger applied first pressure. I was still waiting for the moment when the roundels would become bigger than the sighting-circle . . . then the first burst spurted blazing into the night. I was blinded by the flash and lost sight of the enemy.

A gigantic shadow grew out of the night before me, seemed as though it would seize hold of me—then swept away above my head. I shivered: Mosquito! The sinister word stuck in my mind. Where was it now?

I pulled my aircraft sharply round—there it was, flying straight at me! I realized the other had throttled back, that his speed was reduced. The broad flat shoulders of the Mosquito shone out—offering a good target. The enemy was approaching with his nose pointing away to the left.

The propeller of his left engine was no longer turning. The Tommies were trying to slip away in the darkness, flying close above the ground. I sat on their tail and once more took first pressure, aiming at the right engine. But the machine disappeared in the mist over some low ground.

For a while I searched for a possible damaged enemy aircraft, but then let him off and looked once more for the line of my course on 45°.

Yet, as I looked back, insects were flying against the moon's disc as though attracted to the light: Mosquitoes, coming to help their brother by stinging me. Once again I pressed the throttle lever right forward through the gate. My engine sucked in its petrol thirstily as if overcome with my own horror.

But soon only the rhythm of my pulse still bore witness to the danger come and gone.

Far off sparkled the Maas, the outpost of my homeland. Away in the east, searchlights were nervously
fingering the night sky, here and there drawing across
a silvery point: enemy bombers. Flares appeared
suddenly beyond them, hanging above the landscape,
and reddish-gold spots standing out against the night
sky.

Lüttich slid away beneath me: heavy bombers were
attacking Köln or Aachen. It must actually have been
Aachen, for some minutes afterwards the burning town
lay below me to my right. And then—a group of search-
light beams steadied blindingly on me.

At first I didn't take them seriously and dived down
to escape their troublesome attentions. But then shells
began to fly up, bursting right in front of me. The flak
had gone mad, firing on its own side! I turned my aircraft on its side and flew for a minute into the darkness
before resuming my course. But the Aachen searchlights' fingers were still groping for me. It wouldn't
surprise me if they gave Düsseldorf an air-raid warning—
"Single fast aircraft flying direction Aachen!"

I called up Düsseldorf. The airfield was a large one
and I knew it well.

"*Take care. Night-fighters in the area!*" was the reply.
And now below me the curves of the Rhine were shining
—the airfield lay on the northern edge of the town, not
far from the river.

I "rumbled in" on a wide curve, losing height slowly.
I could easily make out the wide, bare surface of the airfield, but the moonlight was too feeble to allow a proper
estimate of height for the last few metres before landing.

"*Request landing lights.*"

"*Permission not granted. Air-raid warning in force.*"

"*Request lights for a few seconds only,*" I asked.

But they wouldn't allow a single bulb to be switched on. The ground came swiftly up towards me, and it swept into my mind what Ulrich always said about a landing—that it was like sitting in a car weighing eighty hundredweight with two fixed wheels in front and a very small moveable wheel behind, and then having to drive at a speed of nearly two hundred kilometres an hour across rough ground. This time it was night into the bargain, and there would certainly be freshly filled-in bomb-craters.

How high was I? Ten or fifty metres, or only one? A dark wall ahead of me grew thicker and higher—the hangars and the trees on the far side. I cut my throttle, and drew the stick carefully back towards me. The wheels struck heavily and left again with a great bound. This giant's leap mustn't last more than three seconds, or I should crash. I counted—two—three—four—five, and again we rebounded heavily. I raised my arm before my face as my aircraft ran onward along the ground, swung through a complete circle, and came to rest with the left wheel buckled under it.

"We'll certainly need a day on that!" said the chief mechanic.

CHAPTER XV

I WALKED through the town as if I were on leave, for my squadron had already flown on north. The streets were empty and desolate, and the moon cast a pattern of pale light and ghastly shadow across the ruined houses. Here and there I would stumble into a bomb-crater or be brought up sharp by a heap of rubbish. Flak was firing somewhere far away, and from time to time the roar of enemy bombers echoed through the ruins. A soldier such as I, who returns to his homeland after a long while away, wants to see people who don't wear uniform, who yet speak German. My steps rang feebly between the front walls of burnt-out buildings, against the roar of gunfire and the deep tones of bomber engines.

I looked up into the night sky. Up there searchlights trained from all sides had built a pillared cathedral of light, its spire grazing the illuminated belly and broad wings of a Lancaster, set off by a circlet of bursting shells. Red and white incandescent flares appeared suddenly in space, motionless above the deathly streets. Something had begun to bubble and gurgle up there in the air.

"Into the cellar!" someone behind me screamed, and I ran back. But bombs were already bursting a few hundred yards to one side. The tall, empty walls rocked, stones dropping off them, while a rain of thousands of splinters came singing and clattering down as I flung myself through the door of a large house.

Inside, the eyes of women, children and old men gazed at me from beneath the low shored-up ceiling of the air-raid shelter. I was almost ashamed of myself for going in, as a notice above the doorway read:

"Men between sixteen and sixty should be in action, not in a shelter!"

They started talking furiously among themselves, but it didn't worry me, for the next wave of bombs was whistling down, and the talk died away. The suspense lasted seconds only, but they were like an eternity. An old woman began to pray aloud. Close beneath the roof of the shelter, on the topmost of the row of bunks, lay a girl of about sixteen. She held a book in her hand, and her green eyes were gazing at me. A mother drew the head of her young son beneath her apron.

The first bomb burst. And the second—closer. The very foundations of the great house rocked, compressed air was blown and then sucked with an uncanny hollow note through the keyhole in the armoured door. The third bomb was making a rushing noise as it fell. It would certainly hit the house! We all knew it would.

The girl's green eyes were boring stonily into mine. The rushing noise had become like the brushing wing beats of a gigantic bat. I was frightened, frightened of that girl's eyes—they hurt me physically.

A concussion—the splintering of wood and a muffled rumble in the house next door.

We waited.

The sixteen-year-old flung her arms before her face, her slim, manicured fingers digging into her bare shoulders in her terror.

Still we waited.

"Dud," said the old shelter warden.

The mothers and children began to cry—and the girl on the bunk went on with her book.

I got ready to leave.

"You must stay here in the shelter," the old man in the steel helmet advised. "There'll be phosphorus in a moment." I submitted. An old woman called at me.

"Well, you there, we too are in the front line! But if I were as young as you I wouldn't be skulking in a shelter."

The warden broke in.

"Don't you say anything about our friend here. He's already done his duty." And he pointed expressively to my decorations.

"Oh, that's all very fine," the old woman continued maliciously, "but what's he in?"

"Airman!" the other returned. I was red with embarrassment, but it wasn't finished yet. All eyes were focused on me.

"Then get back up there again!" resounded from the back of the room.

"He's on leave, I expect," the shelter warden defended me.

"No," I said firmly. "I'm only trained for day fighting."

"Only for day-fighting?" repeated the old woman. "Well, that's our leaders' fault again!"

But that was too much for the worthy warden.

"Now kindly be quiet, *liebe Frau*. The 'high-ups' know quite well how our fighters should go into action. The Führer knows all about it"—he raised his voice as he finished.

"What do you mean—Führer!" shouted the old woman. "Here we are—dying in this cellar, and those high-ups . . . they ought to put every one of them against a wall, the traitors!"

Everyone had heard the old woman's furious outburst, and a middle-aged civilian pushed forward from the background.

"That kind of talk against our leaders will cost you dear!" An icy silence had spread across the room.

"She's seventy-six," the warden observed mildly.

"Her age makes no difference," the other angrily retorted. I was just about to break in myself, when the old woman began mumbling,

"Why now, Herr Blockleiter, I haven't said anything wrong. On the contrary, I asked the young soldier to shoot the bombers down, and I wished that they could put all of them up there against a wall, those bombers high up there above us"—she concluded with emphasis.

Loud laughter resounded on all sides. "Good for her!" some called out. "Yes, that's what she said," others cried.

The civilian swore and went back to his place.

"Phosphorus coming!"

The cry ran suddenly through the room, as though to announce the plague or a flood. Someone or other must have seen it falling outside. "Dropping further over towards the Rhine, towards the old town."

Thousands of cases of liquid flame were indeed smashing down there through the roofs and exploding everywhere, white-hot liquid flowing in blinding streams down walls and staircases, swathing everything in fire, blocking exits from cellars and streets. The next moment the high wind was carrying the flames across whole districts while blazing human figures scurried frantically round or were baked to cinders beneath collapsing masonry.

Several women began again to mutter prayers, but these grew softer and then ceased altogether. Everyone held their breath. The warden clenched his teeth, his jawbones forced outwards, sweat running over his forehead beneath the steel helmet. Looking at me, he brought his mouth close to my ear to whisper something. But he didn't speak. Something was clattering and splashing against the house walls and in the roof timbers, as though great hailstones were rebounding from the tiles.

"Here they come," a woman shrieked in terror, "our house is on fire!"

At the same time something roared all around us, the foundations quaked beneath our feet, ceiling and walls apparently about to collapse on us. The bomb in the house next door had burst. There was a rumble of falling brick.

"That was no dud," the warden murmured.

"Jesus help us! Jesus!" a young woman was screaming shrilly across the room. Everyone was crowding—fighting his way towards the exit. The old man in the steel helmet vainly tried to restrain them, but his voice did not reach the woman who was now trying to force her way past us, still screaming, her eyes glassy. I caught her in my arms, and then I saw that she was going to have a baby—and now. The first discharge was running down her legs.

"Oh God," she groaned, "help me!"

"We'll help you," I said as I laid her on a mattress. The shelter had emptied except for the old woman and the warden.

"There's a doctor next door," the old man gasped, and I ran off. The way into the next house must be right under the staircase. A man was standing there with a pocket-torch.

"Where's the doctor?"

"I'm a doctor," he replied, without looking up. Two men were crawling through the hole in the connecting wall.

"Come with me!" I yelled. "There's a woman having a baby."

"I'm not coming," the other replied, his voice toneless. The arms of a third man were reaching from the cellar on the other side. "Where are my children? Where is my wife?" the doctor moaned, and he began calling out their names through the gap.

"Here we are! We're coming," a voice from the cellar answered. I took hold of the man in the cellar-entrance—immediately above him the cellar roof was carrying the whole weight of the burning house.

"Oh dear, my new jacket!" a woman's voice down below in the darkness exclaimed. Others could be heard there, cursing and weeping.

Then everything collapsed in front of us. As the great weight of the ceiling bore down on them, there were a few last screams. After that not a gurgle emerged from the buried basement.

The man in the entrance was clutching hold of me. His legs had been crushed. I had got a poor grip of him and could hold on no longer. He tried to use his legs to kick himself out, but they were useless and he knew it. He looked at me with wide, sad eyes and a faint smile, as though he were mildly offended by something. And then he let himself slip back into the cellar entrance—still smiling sadly to the last—and the rest of the roof slid rattling after him.

It was only then I realized what had happened. The doctor beside me was hammering on the massive communicating wall and trying to dig into the mortar with a penknife. Then he stopped and listened. Knocking was coming from the other side, so there must be someone still alive.

Eventually helpers arrived. Pickaxes flew, but the wall was too strong for them. Firemen began trying to put out the flames, but the smoking ruins absorbed huge quantities of water. It was all useless. But down there in the cellar hope still survived somehow—someone was still going on knocking. Yet we knew that within an hour they would all be dead—crushed, stifled, burnt or drowned. . . .

From far behind us in the shelter the screams of the woman in labour reached us, her pains following one another at shorter and shorter intervals. The doctor at my side was staring at the ground and I took hold of his shoulder to console him.

"Shouldn't we get her away?"

"No," he replied, unable to keep back his tears. "I'm coming. Get some water."

As we entered the shelter the man in the steel helmet told us it might be hours yet before the house above us would be burnt out.

"Clean water," the doctor repeated, and the warden went off to fetch it.

"She's having them every five minutes now," the old woman croaked, while the young one lying there kept screaming, her fingers clutching my arm. Then the screams sank to a groan and it was quiet again.

The doctor looked at his watch, and his left cheek twitched as someone knocked again on the other side of the cellar wall. In there they were still alive and hoping.

Staring at the wall, "I can't do any more," he sobbed aloud. "My wife and children are dying in there!"

However, the warden was back now with a bucket of water and a towel, and the doctor began fumbling in his bag, his tears dropping on the scissors which he had laid out ready. Now he drew on his gloves.

"Hold her," he told me, and I knelt down and took her arms. Her shrieks resounding through the damp cellar and re-echoing horribly, she kept twisting about in her agony. Gradually, though, she calmed down and her body lay bared. The doctor looked at his watch again and put his stethoscope against the tensed abdomen. Then he gave the labouring woman an injection, and felt the head of the unborn child.

"It's coming now," he told her. "When you cry out, you must press with all your force down on your abdomen. And you," he whispered across to me, "pull her legs up and part them a bit."

He kept wiping his face free of the tears and sweat.

So for the first time I witnessed the birth of a human being. I had been afraid it would make me sick, but instead the solemnity of it steadied me, a sense of miracle . . .

As she groaned, the infant was pressed lower and lower and her body began to open—to a tiny creature setting out on its own path, for the four of us an embodiment of the power and splendour of life.

The baby's head and black hair were already visible, and the doctor gathered his fingers carefully around it. The labouring woman groaned once more, and the head slipped from her body. The tiny head had gone blue, seemed to be lifeless, for the umbilical cord had looped itself round its neck and was throttling it.

"Don't press any more," the doctor called. I held my breath, fearing the worst. The old woman was staring wide-eyed from her corner. In the cellar of the house next door the dying were knocking afresh. The doctor pressed his lips together, and the veins stood out on his forehead.

I thought, "He can't fail now."

The scissor-blades gripped the umbilical cord, and the next moment he had cut it through.

"Now press!" he cried. The small creature's shoulder was already thrusting out. The doctor quickly grasped the tiny arm, drew it out, and the child glided from its mother's body—a boy. The newest of creatures hung from the doctor's hand, its head down like a skinned hare, its skin smeared with a thin coating of pale cream. The wonderful thing, beyond all this world's planners, had happened: a complete human being, with arms, legs, head and all its senses had been born.

There we were still fearing for the life of this baby boy, while a few yards from us, just behind the communicating wall, life was being extinguished. Again and again the doctor slapped the back of the newly born, and now— there was a rattling, the first sound of a tiny voice. It was still crying plaintively as the doctor washed the small body and wrapped it in the towel.

Morning was breaking. But daylight glimmered through only now and then, as the wind shifted; a thick curtain of vapour lay across the town, the black smoke hanging low in the streets.

I went to Hinterschallers's house, passing close to the Altstadt. Far off I could see the reddish-yellow gleams of the conflagration. Lost children were running sobbing through the smoke, among charred fragments of paper and ash whirling to the ground. Moaning women, mothers searching for their lost, were stumbling over the burnt-out ruins, often with their solitary possession, a soaking blanket, held as protection against the heat. A few firemen were doing their best, but their efforts were pitiable against such a furnace.

I turned off into a side street where there stood a dustman's lorry. Men with great forks and shovels, men with heavy gloves, were heaping small black corpses on to it.

"Are they all children?" I asked, in horror.

"No, *junger Herr*," answered one of them with a kind of brutish seriousness. "They were once upon a time all the same size as you; one metre seventy, one metre eighty, and more," he ended as if he were at an auction. I felt sick, and hurried on so as not to see the charred bodies any more. But they were lying around everywhere: small, black and shrunken, already swollen up—like dwarf negroes. There was a sweet smell in the air. But I had to breathe, and if I had closed my eyes I should certainly have fallen.

The people lying there had only died a few hours previously; burnt-out ruins where the phosphorus had overwhelmed them as they were leaving their houses— in cellar entrances where the outside air had shrivelled them up as they tried to escape from the inferno within— in the middle of the streets, where the steam from their soaking blankets had scalded them to death as they struggled to get away under them between conflagrations —on the edges of pavements where they had been burnt up as with seared faces they tried to wet themselves with what slight moisture remained in the gutters—down sewer manholes where they plunged again and again into the scalding water till the flames consumed the last oxygen and they floated unconsciously away. . . .

They are too much for us, I thought, and too many. But the bombers will get what's coming to them—now more than ever!

CHAPTER XVI

THE howl of the sirens woke us, as the first raids of the evening were reported.

"We must go down into the cellar," Danielle said. She had been allowed to have the bed belonging to Hinterschallers's landlord, who now got up, grumbling angrily, from our place on the carpet to switch on the light.

"*Liebes Fräulein—Mademoiselle*—I have been living here for twenty years without having been hit by a bomb. I'm going to brew a pot of coffee."

But Danielle was frightened. "I can hear the noise of an engine quite clearly. Listen!"

"Yes, I can hear a noise. They ought to give it some of my Ex-pastilles! You know my slogan, don't you? 'Take Hinterschallers's Ex-tablets, and your wind will ne'er go free—involuntarily!'"

Danielle laughed dutifully, although she didn't really know how to take it.

"But suppose the bombers are aiming at this house at this moment?"

"The name of my firm is on the roof in large illuminated letters, and there is a good business friend of mine, one of my representatives, sitting in the Air Ministry in London. He has instructed all pilots not to hit my house. Now do you feel better?"

So we were soon sitting round the small table, the droning of enemy bombers getting further and further away. Hinterschallers had put on a civvy suit, and looked almost presentable.

"They won't do anything to us here." And, indicating his suit, he added, "You see, they don't drop bombs on the civil population."

Danielle shook her head—her road also had taken her through the burnt-out Altstadt.

"It's horrible. I never believed such ghastliness could exist." As we said nothing she continued sadly, "I'm afraid the whole object of my journey has now gone too."

"What do you mean? You'll see Ulrich again all right —you'll be with him as far as the pearly gates, and what happens after that, heaven knows."

"Yes, I'll see Ulrich again. I'll be able to fill out the memory I have of him. But that will be worse, perhaps, than if I had been able to forget him in Perpignan. I didn't want to come to him, to see him again, because I'm prepared to wait. I want to save him—though I see now why he is fighting. But I know now that he is not doing what I begged him to do."

"You'll be with Ulrich to-morrow," I said. "And if he has you near him he won't take so many risks. He's an old fox and knows exactly where the dangers and the chances lie."

Her mind was gradually set at rest, and Hinterschallers now began telling the story of their journey.

"They nearly finished us off an hour beyond Laon. Mosquitoes, of course, a whole crowd of them at intervals of a minute or two. First they flew down the road and then back. There were tanks in front of us and tanks behind. One of the Tommies dropped three parachute flares right over our heads. Now we're for it, I thought. But man proposes, God disposes—in the end they went off without firing a shot."

"What time was that?" I asked, casually.

"Just when it had got dark. Heaven knows why they didn't attack—perhaps they saw who I was."

"I know why," I said, and the two of them looked up. "At the same time and place a German fighter attacked one of those Mosquitoes, and a few minutes afterwards quite half a dozen of them collected in order to establish my identity."

"What do you mean—*your* identity?"

"Oh, I only wanted to try shooting one of them down at night."

"Just a moment!" cried Hinterschallers, springing to his feet and rummaging in a box. There was the pop of a cork. "Cognac. The very best! Let's all have a nip. And now for a description of the fight. Make it as dangerous and exciting as you can. It's so safe in here," he ended luxuriously.

But with each glass Danielle grew sadder.

"I don't think you have exaggerated your description. But all the time I can't help thinking of Ulrich. He, too, has to go through these terrible fights. I feel it'll happen to him, too, one of these days, as it has to all the others. I already know the sound of it before they tell me— 'Ulrich has been killed!' And then shall I go back to France—perhaps as a traitor? No, I won't go back there."

"I don't really think, Danielle, you could ever stop Ulrich from flying. You've seen the ruins and all the devastation in the Altstadt. You'll see the same picture all over Germany. We know that now it is up to each and every one of us, and that every time a bomber is shot down more human lives will be saved."

"But you can't win the war now!" she cried, with a break in her voice.

"That's got nothing to do with it," I replied. I wanted to tell her about the doctor whose wife and children had been burnt to death within a few yards of him while he helped an unknown baby into the world. But I held back. Danielle had had enough.

CHAPTER XVII

HINTERSCHALLERS had just served the main course when George came in. Seeing this almost forgotten victim of misfortune actually standing in the doorway, we could hardly believe our eyes. George didn't move a muscle as he stood before the Kapitän.

"Reporting back from operations. One Boeing rammed."

The Chief, who in point of fact didn't know him, but had heard the whole calamitous story, rose smiling to his feet.

"Hardly worth mentioning, I suppose, that you have been lying in hospital for several months since?"

After that he shook hands and invited him to the table. Hands reached over from all directions to shake his as he returned to sit among us again: with a flattened nose, a set of artificial teeth like most of the older of us had, a grey strand of hair combed back off his forehead and— as we soon noticed—a distinctly "cracked head."

"This afternoon is a free-for-all after low-flying aircraft," the Kapitän was telling him. "The squadron's two thousandth aircraft is shortly to be shot down!"

George plucked up courage.

"Request permission, Herr Hauptmann, to take off with you."

The Kapitän wrinkled his brow.

"My dear fellow, you've only just come out of hospital, and you haven't flown for some time. I don't know whether I can approve it, particularly as the Kommandeur grounded you before your last operation. You know quite well that disobedience of orders like that is a court-martial offence."

George looked down dejectedly. We were thinking the same as he was—he must fly again! Papi looked at the Hauptmann for a long, a very long time, and the Chief took the hint.

"Very well," he said, "I'll give the Kommandeur a ring. I'll do my best."

So George flew with us after all, and was the first to sight the enemy. He chased the low-flying Americans—ahead of all of us—got the last one in his sights, fired, and the two-thousandth squadron victory was his. We had taken off in company with several other flights and were still chasing some Yanks. Great attention had to be given to the landscape as it whipped past only a few metres beneath us. Trees, houses, and high-tension wires called for caution, as they had to be cleared at exactly the right moment. Every second drove us more than a hundred and fifty metres onwards, and a small incorrect pressure forward on the stick meant a crash and certain death.

Ulrich was flying his aircraft close beside mine. His machine lay like a bright "something" at the edge of my range of vision, and this light-coloured patch kept company with me like a phantom, sometimes moving up for a moment, sometimes dropping back. It wasn't easy to keep charge of one's thoughts and eyes in these conditions. One's eyes were straining ahead, but they had still to be vigilant and controlled. It was vitally important to keep glancing down at the ribbon of approaching landscape as it practically grazed the aircraft and hurtled away astern, but tempting, too, to look across at the next man and exchange a quick greeting. I knew well that Ulrich wanted to do the same, now that the Americans had disappeared from sight.

I decided I would permit myself a quick look across, and so pulled my aircraft up a few feet to a safe height— Ulrich was crouched in his narrow cockpit, leaning slightly forward, where I could make him out as plainly as if he were sitting with me and drinking a cup of coffee. He still didn't look up, though he had seen I was looking at him. At last his head jerked round towards me, he nodded, his mouth grinned cheerfully then he moved his head back as quickly as it had come, in the direction in which our two-thousand-horse-power machines were carrying us.

It could only have been the fraction of a second, but just that interval made it too late for Ulrich to see the fateful obstruction ahead. In the second as he looked forward again at the landscape rushing towards him, his machine grazed the top of a tree. The left wing rose with a gentle movement and the aircraft began to bank steeper and steeper. Looking in horror at the distorted face of my friend, I realized at once what had happened. His machine was damaged and no longer responded to his will. If only for a moment, Friend Hein was now at the controls, and in this moment I was looking at Death, and Ulrich knew it too.

Though he was still hoping desperately against hope, it was too late. Gradually, as if in slow-motion, the aircraft turned on to its back and Ulrich's fate was sealed.

The machine struck the ground, exploded and dissolved into a thousand white-hot fragments, a huge mushroom-column of smoke and fire shooting up high in the air in the centre of our formation. My heart was beating wildly, and driving a wave of nausea into my throat. But I had to overcome my pain alone, and with it the feeling that I was partly to blame. I had to keep cool and calm, had to keep my eyes looking straight ahead and not behind to where a few seconds before Ulrich had been torn into shreds.

Seconds meant kilometres, and a minute a dozen of them: time and distance drew us further and further away from his life and from the tattered fragments of his body.

Several aircraft were flying astern of me and had got restless. They hadn't seen the cause of the crash. One had already asked whether enemy fighters had attacked. I had to set his mind at rest in a few words. So I just said, "It's nothing," into the mouthpiece of my radio, in a voice as dull as I could make it.

I taxied up to my hangar as if in a dream and climbed numbly from the cockpit. Danielle was waiting beside Ulrich's hangar, and I walked slowly towards her. She must have realized all too well what I had to say. We looked at one another for a long while until she began to tremble, her distress calling out at me from her wide open eyes—until I couldn't bear her look any longer and dropped my own to the ground.

"It's my fault," I said.

"No," she said. Then she turned like a flash and ran.

"Danielle!" I called, in an effort to fetch her back. But she wouldn't listen and kept running faster still right across the field, where the landing aircraft were still coming in. In this blind, deaf state she soon disappeared into the thicket on the far side.

When I got to barracks I found her room empty. Her red shawl was lying where she had left it, and I took it away with me, for Ulrich.

There was not very much left of our friend. One bare yellowish thighbone with some charred tatters of flesh

was all that could be found amid the burnt-out wreckage
and scorched earth.

That was what we had to bury.

The padre's words were familiar to us, for we heard
them frequently enough. They didn't worry us in our
thoughts of the dead man, for whose fate I had been
partly to blame. Still, I knew he would pronounce me
innocent, if only he were able—that he, the wanderer
from another world, was smiling as he continued his
journey, on to other stars. . . .

I kept searching in my mind for the face of my dead
friend and the qualities which I connected with the sound
of his name. I tried to remember movements associated
with him alone, characteristic of him, the tone of his voice,
or his laugh. But it was in vain. At these very moments
I most wanted to devote to him, neither desire nor memory
could evoke a really clear enough picture. At least, I
thought, if I could see his face, I should perhaps be
able to recapture his voice, and to see and hear his
laughter.

As the coffin sank into the ground and I still could not
so much as imagine my friend, my confusion and distress
were fearful.

Volleys of rifle-shots shattered my thoughts. Someone
there in front was again reciting words no doubt used at
every funeral, as shovelfuls of earth fell muffled and hollow
on the coffin. Why must all this be gone through?
These orations for the departed, on the transitoriness of
man, this funereal music and this final hollow thud? All
simply to increase the pain, deepen the realization of
never seeing him again—never again! Why couldn't
strangers bury Ulrich's body, and I delude myself that
he be living on? Why not, instead of walking to the
grave, to the resting place of a rotting corpse, with nothing

in common with the Ulrich I knew, why not deny his death? No, so long as I was alive, Ulrich was alive too.

I had hoped to see Danielle by the grave. But she wasn't to be found anywhere, not even when the congregation's last steps had fallen silent along the gravel paths of the cemetery. I could well understand her not coming, it was perhaps a good thing—both that, and that I should not see her again.

I went with Werner to the unassuming grey house beside the town church. The old organist knew us and so he knew what to do when we asked him. We listened to Bach. If heaven existed, it was in this music.

CHAPTER XVIII

WEEKS had passed since Ulrich's crash, and the poor state of our morale was making things even gloomier, many of us only wishing the autumn would put an end to it all.

The front was actually still able to hold the assault back from the frontiers of the Reich, but the rear-services were going more and more to pieces.

Day by day our air operations were becoming more difficult, the enemy superiority having risen immeasurably, and our formation returning home seldom without losses—only occasionally would one of us climb smiling from his cockpit. The mechanics stuck as well as ever to their jobs, making good by their efforts the failings of manufacturers or the shortcomings of inadequate supply. The belief these fellows in their black overalls still had in victory and their hope of a miracle weapon which should turn the scales gave them the strength to go on, the youngest of them trying every means of getting to active service at the front. But, needed here as they were, I couldn't help feeling sorry for them with their conviction that they were being prevented from saving their Fatherland, National-Socialist Germany, from being delivered to an enemy who was going to destroy everything, rape the women and children, castrate the men and dismember German Kultur.

While the Allied bombers were staging what almost amounted to a fly-past, and endless squadrons of Americans flew above our heads, we—a hundred German pilots—could only stand around beside our aircraft and their generally empty petrol tanks.

A combined operation for all north-German fighters, however, had been in preparation for weeks past. Reichsmarschall Goering intended to show we were still capable of destroying whole formations of bombers in the space of a few minutes.

I walked with Werner across the tarmac. I often thought about Ulrich and Danielle, and about my promise to look after her. But I hadn't heard anything more from her, and that grieved and hurt me. Why hadn't she stayed, seeing that her road back to France was cut off? I had already so often longed for her to come back, and now I was realizing more and more that this longing sprang not only from the memory of my promise.

"Where can Danielle have got to?" I couldn't help wondering aloud, really simply to hear the sound of her name again.

Werner looked surprised.

"What's the point of thinking about that? The girl was pretty impossible."

"Still, they were very much in love. He did want to marry her."

"How do you know that?"

"I couldn't help overhearing one of their conversations."

"Danielle hated us Germans."

"She hated the 'Hitlers,'" I corrected him. "Ulrich didn't have much time either for the hundred-and-fifty percenters."

Werner was biting his lip, as he always did when he was embarrassed or angry. I took him by the shoulder.

"Now listen to me, old fellow! You're a faithful pimp of the Führer's, whatever you may say. But Ulrich was against the war and against Hitler."

"Why talk such nonsense? What did Ulrich die for, then?"

"He died for something else, Werner. Not so much for 'Führer, People and Fatherland' as simply for 'People and Fatherland.'"

"It can't be split up like that," Werner replied, "the Führer's the embodiment of our philosophy of life, in which we're all indissolubly joined."

"You've got that nicely by heart, my dear fellow. Ulrich said to me once that there was something wrapped up with the name of Hitler which had nothing whatsoever to do with the name of the German people."

"What do you mean by that?"

"What I want to say is something that never gets said except behind locked doors—that mass-murderers have been at work for a long time past in Poland and even on German soil, criminals whose tasks and uniforms have been provided by Hitler.

Werner was becoming aggressive. "This damned shit-house talk! You never hear it out in the open. Look here, man, what you're saying is just nothing. You simply don't seem to understand. To-day's problem is quite different—it's a matter of life and death for a whole people—our people!"

"So Ulrich *is* right!"

"Nonsense. You're not one of us any longer!"

We had arrived in front of our aircraft. Ten or twenty engines had already started up all around us, and hundreds of aircraft were climbing into the air as we, too, took off.

"*Fly course north, height seven thousand*," came the order from the ground, and the Commodore turned carefully with the whole squadron in the new direction.

Soon the altimeter was showing four thousand metres.

Werner was flying close alongside me, with his oxygen mask on—I usually put mine on when the engine's supercharger cut in automatically as we reached the necessary height. The aircraft would then shake violently and remind me to adjust my mask. It was dangerous to forget it, for as you got higher and higher the air became thinner every minute without your realizing it. In the end a pleasant languor would come over you, or else you would get mildly intoxicated and start to laugh and sing, unconscious of danger. By that time the ability to think logically would already have been lost, and you would either fall asleep or collapse suddenly over the stick as if struck by a blow. Many chaps crashed to their death in this way, and either they never woke up or only just before hitting the ground—still numbed and powerless.

"Circle!"

The order shook me from my meditations. We were flying at seven thousand metres and still I hadn't put the thing on! As I drew the oxygen deep into my lungs the first thin veil of height-sickness was withdrawn, and my sight and thoughts grew clear again.

Our fighter armada was wheeling in great circles above a north German town, its ruins unidentifiable at this distance. Circling meant waiting—waiting for other squadrons which were to join us to-day in attacking the giant bombers.

But neither friend nor foe was to be seen. The North Sea lay shimmering on the horizon and a slight mist hid objects at a great distance. We were still circling, and forty minutes had already gone by since take-off when a second squadron came up from the south to join us. More than two hundred aircraft were now waiting for a third and a fourth formation—and then for the enemy.

Fresh orders arrived ceaselessly, to fly on a new course, change height, and wait. We soon released our empty long-range tanks and switched over to our own. Someone had turned the wrong cock and was gliding down with his engine dead, and a second, who may well have been overcome by the height, was reeling and mumbling in the rear.

"About a hundred Boeings to the northward of us!" called the Commodore.

Our eyes rested intently on the mighty flying citadels. Through half-closed eyes they would look like silvery sheep with dogs chivvying them on all sides, guarding the flock as it moved slowly onwards towards its objective. The shining bodies and wings, and the bombers' glassed-in turrets sparkled and shone beneath the sun's rays. They must have sighted us by now.

"*Wait!*" ordered our control on the ground. We had all switched on our sights and gun-circuits so as to be ready to open fire at any moment. Every one of us must have been gripped by the lust for the chase, but still our orders came—"*Wait!*"

"A soldier spends half his life waiting," someone exclaimed.

"Shut your mouth!" someone else retorted nervily, and a general stream of anathema followed. We were all fed up with these crazy orders which made us stay waiting while the bombers were already losing height here in front of us. Our third and fourth squadrons were no-where to be seen.

"Request permission to attack with our two for-mations!" the Commodore asked.

"*Not approved. Wait! . . . Pour me another coffee.*" In the control-room at the ground headquarters they had forgotten to switch off their transmitter.

"Don't swallow it the wrong way!" a pilot called maliciously.

"We can't wait any longer. Our tanks'll be empty in half an hour."

"*I'll court-martial you if you don't obey orders!*" shouted the ground-controller, who had himself never been a fighter-pilot.

"Do whatever you have to!" replied our Commodore angrily. "Down we go, boys, we'll attack! Second squadron engage the fighter-escort!"

"*I'll court-martial you . . . !*" came a last wrathful expostulation from the ground. But up here everyone was choosing his position in the wide line of attack, two hundred pairs of eyes staring along the sights, hands firmly on stick and throttle lever, thumb and index-finger on the firing buttons.

I had stayed alongside Werner and cast a quick glance across at him—as he looked round at the same instant, our eyes met. The face behind the goggles, helmet and snouted mask was frightening. Meanwhile the four-engined monsters were growing larger as we drove down on them.

"The third from the right," Werner said.

I took station five hundred metres astern of him to follow up on his attack without delay.

"*Achtung!* Spitfires and Thunderbolts attacking from above!"

The warning had come too late. We were already in range of the cross-fire from the bombers, within which they were almost safe from enemy fighters. Werner lay ahead of me, right in the hail of fire from the rear-guns. Then he tipped forward and dived vertically downwards.

Now they had shifted their fire to me. I grasped the stick with both hands and the six-fold chains of blazing metal spurted from my guns, pouring their hundreds of shots into the huge fortress in front of me, crackling through the thin aluminium behind which nine men believed they were doing their duty like me. Nine! Some with fair or dark hair, brown or blue eyes, small snub noses and large feet, gold teeth, rings on their fingers, and wallets with pictures and letters from wives and children. A few minutes before they had opened their bomb-doors and killed innumerable human beings, who knew joys and sorrows just as they did themselves. And now I was firing—mutilating the heads, eyes, feet, hands, teeth, and photographs scarcely fifty paces in front of me!

The rear-gunner is hit and is hanging bloodily in his harness, his four-barrelled gun staring downwards, silent and motionless. I can see no more enemies in my sights. Perhaps they're all dead—all except the pilot, desperately holding his machine in the air.

The box over there is carrying eight bodies through the air! I don't want to shoot into dead flesh any longer, I don't want to any more! My fingers leave the firing-buttons and the guns go silent.

What ought I to do now?

I hold on helplessly behind the bomber—but something is moving in the turret. The man I thought dead is raising his arm and staring at me. One of his comrades is trying to drag him out of his harness, and he, too, is staring at me in the same horror from behind his breathing-mask. Take it easy, take it easy, old fellow, I think, just get your friend away out of it—he hasn't got to go on staring at my threatening guns—I won't fire at you.

But now one of them's training his guns on me once more.

"Take your fingers off it, you idiot!" I roar.

But the fellow there in front of me can't hear—and I'm

quicker than him. I touch the firing-button with one finger—and his gun-turret is shattered. Pieces of metal fly past, striking against my machine. Then the whole rear gun-position breaks away and plunges into the depths below.

Now I can see right through the hollow body of the aircraft into the pilot's cabin. The pilot, sitting in front of his armour protection, still won't tell his crew to jump. Doubtless he's thinking of the wounded. But then I think of the thousands of human beings lying amid the burning ruins of our towns, and I know that this bomber will come back again with a new load of death.

I clench my teeth and hurl my bursts of steel into the defenceless flying coffin until it dips its nose forward and—hurtles earthwards.

All this could only have lasted half a minute, but for me it was an eternity from which I had now been torn. The bomber formation was already far away in front, though fighters—friend and foe—were banking and looping wildly all around me. Green and red tracer, criss-crossing the turmoil, marked the streams of gunfire, and here and there a flaming or smoking aircraft would spin down out of the fight. It was a miracle I had not yet been shot down myself. But as I glanced to one side the miracle explained itself—Werner was flying watchfully beside me—yes, actually keeping an eye on me.

"Let's have another go at the Boeings," he suggested. I opened my throttle wide. This time Werner stayed behind in the second position, nearly a kilometre astern.

"*Achtung!*" he called. "Fly straight ahead! There's a Tommy on your tail. He's in my sights."

This was a moment when it paid to have nerves of steel. An enemy fighter, which might not have seen Werner, had moved in between us. Astern of me an enemy was already taking aim, and it was up to me to stay quietly along the line of his sights to make sure Werner should have a safe target!

The Englishman was approaching closer and closer, and in a few moments he would open fire. You don't belong to us any longer, Werner had said. The thought passed quickly through my mind—if he were a devil, he would let the Englishman fire at me. "You don't belong to us any longer!"

The enemy had come in to a distance of four hundred metres. Werner was asking too much. No, he mightn't really be a devil: but a gun-stoppage or an unsure hand could ruin everything. My nerves gave way—weren't they going to be ripped to shreds anyway in a few seconds?

I hauled the stick round, and at the same instant the Englishman was shattered by Werner's fire.

When we had both landed and climbed out of our aircraft we stood for a moment looking at one another.

"Thanks," Werner said.

A long way off Hinterschallers was shouting. "Congratulations, *meine Herren*! And were the *Herren* troubled by wind on the way up?"

We smiled.

CHAPTER XIX

IN the last days of November thick layers of fog were lying over the north German moorlands. But whenever the weather was clear we could make out the countless condensation trails—token of their mastery of the air—with which the Allied squadrons continuously criss-crossed the sky.

No one was talking in the control-room; everyone waiting for a word from the Fighter-General who was now sitting on a wooden bench among us. He seemed to have aged since his previous visit, although he was still only about thirty. As always, he held a cigar between half-open lips below his small moustache. We loved him: he was ours! He had risen from our ranks, been decorated with the highest orders and been made the youngest General. But his courage, experience and intelligence had not been given full scope—they would listen in high places to his advice and then not follow it. Build fighters, fighters and still more fighters, he had said—but it was never done. And now, with enemy bombers flying undisturbed in their thousands over our country and reducing our towns to rubble our General had been made responsible for the air-defence of the Reich. But now, of course, they were asking the impossible.

His hand supporting his head, he was looking gloomily in front of him. At last he raised his eyes.

"Well, boys, I just don't know what to do. My influence up there is exhausted and I shall soon be gone. That's how it is." Always brief and to the point, he passed his hand across his forehead and beard. "What was the other thing?—Oh, George, come here!" And as the cadet came forward, "You are transferred to the testing-station for turbine aircraft. I have read your application. But you can't go and fight Johnny. The Reichsmarschall won't allow any private wars in the air."

George stiffened. He didn't want to be transferred: it was a question of the honour of the Abbeville Boys. Less than a week previously he had heard that the best British fighter-pilot had challenged him, the winner of the squadron's two-thousandth victory, to single combat in the air.

It was not for nothing that the evaluating section for enemy propaganda had passed that article from an English newspaper into George's hands. He had read there with his own eyes, "British Ace challenges German Ace"—to which, of course, there was only one answer. (George had previously not replied to the challenge passed over the radio by a British Wing Commander with thirty-five victories to his credit, probably because he did not want to tempt Providence!)

No, George wasn't afraid. He wanted to get going now.

"Well?" asked the General, waiting.

"I must fight Johnny!" he replied gravely. He called the Englishman by his Christian name, and when George used such names he was always referring to a friend— Johnny from the other side must indeed be a friend, ever since this challenge, a worthy friend and opponent, a kind of embodiment of chivalry and fair play.

Our General looked at the cadet sharply and asked, "You are not willing to accept transfer?"

"No!" the other replied, in a firm, clear voice.

The General leapt to his feet and shouted at George, "You're to obey orders!"

"*Jawohl, Herr General!*"

The cadet's resistance had broken. The older man took him by the arm and looked him in the eyes. But when he spoke his voice was soft.

"George, man, I know just how you feel. I'm just the same as you and the rest of us. But listen—let me tell you as an old hand that it's better this way. Apart from that," he added in his ordinary voice and turning away, "apart from that I'll make it my business to see that your court-martial charge is dropped."

After that our General went away, and we never saw him again.

As always happens when senior officers are relieved, the new Commanding Officer wished to do everything he could to demonstrate his own efficiency and that of the unit committed to his charge.

It went like this. On the last day of the year we were called together. Piles of flying-cards, forms and orders lay in front of us, and we had to sign a declaration which pledged us to the greatest secrecy and threatened the death penalty in the event of non-observance. Two thousand German fighter and tactical aircraft—so ran the orders—were to attack the airfields in Belgium and Northern France in the early hours of New Year's Day, when it was supposed that the English and Americans would be in the midst of their New Year celebrations. The attack was to be carried out at ground level with gun armament.

We plodded back to our quarters through the snow with mixed feelings.

But as nearby church bells were ringing in the New Year, we rose from the dinner table and emptied our

glasses to the success of the forthcoming operation. We
pilots, fully aware as we were of the difficulty of the task,
nevertheless had not observed the order to abstain from
all alcohol; we meant to enjoy the pleasures of this world
at least once more. Even the youngest guessed, and the
older knew, that what lay ahead meant that every second
or third man among us would probably lose his life before
morning.

So the hubbub continued, virtually without a pause.
We danced, laughed and drank until quite suddenly—
on a gesture from the Kommandeur—the orchestra
stopped playing: the saxophone's sweet sensual notes
died away, but the drummer, who was dull with drowsi-
ness, continued for a few seconds to beat out his ominous
rhythm. In the sticky silence which followed, one could
almost hear the irregular beating of our hearts. Everyone
knew what was coming might mean goodbye for all of
us, for ever.

"*Meine Herren*," the Kommandeur's voice rang out
across the silent room, "we will check our watches. Take
off in fifty minutes!"

Leaving the girls where they were, we walked in silence
to the cars. There were no heart-rending scenes—
nothing more, perhaps, than a hurried kiss, or a tragic
look exchanged.

While outside on the airfield our aircraft, sixty in all,
stood waiting in the fresh, powdery snow as if on parade,
in the control-room we heard the Kommandeur's final
briefing. It was a small room, and we had to crowd round
the tactical chart to find out what we could about the plan.
Among the unfamiliar faces of several airmen who had
landed here the day before, I noted the child-like features
of a seventeen- or eighteen-year-old and reflected that
some of the new pilots whom the Kommandeur had

brought in for this operation would not return from it either. Perhaps it mightn't be noticed straight away—unfamiliar faces wouldn't be missed. Anyway, I stamped the features of this seventeen-year-old on my mind, to remember him if he didn't come back.

The jazz band in the next room was playing *Blood-red Roses*, and Vogel shouted rudely across at them, "Why not play *Das Lied vom toten Kameraden*?"[1]

The saxophonist glanced up stupidly and broke into *Take it Easy*; the drummer almost dislocating his arms as he raptly hotted up his rhythm.

Changed into our leather flying-suits, we stood drawing nervously at our cigarettes, only Vogel and Meyer II having come on from dinner in their mess-uniforms. These two now climbed into their aircraft in white shirts, patent-leather shoes and white gloves.

"If we have to stay behind on the other side," Vogel called irrepressibly, "the Tommies'll know they have to deal with superior people. Oh yes, they'll admit all right that the Knights of Abbeville are still going strong. What's the Latin for it?"

"X minus thirty," the moment of take-off, was approaching. Photographers from the staff of the *Wochenschau* had been installing automatic cameras in the aircraft of our most expert pilots during the night, and now were standing behind their own mobile cameras, ready to film by artificial light the rare spectacle of a mass take-off by German fighters. The first neighbouring squadrons from the hinterland of Germany were already flying westward at low altitude.

A hundred and twenty thousand horse-power, from sixty aircraft thundered across the airfield, blowing the virgin snow of New Year's Eve into whirling clouds with

[1]*The Dead Comrades' Song.*

their take-off. We were to fly low so as not to be detected by enemy radar—but a safe height was hard to estimate above the bare, greyish-white landscape. Often we would think we were going to graze the earth, till an isolated tree suddenly showed up at least a hundred feet below, or alternatively suppose ourselves at a safe height only to have to pull up in alarm from a haystack. The desolate, snow-grey landscape drew interminably away beneath us, the red and green navigation lights of the other aircraft our only reminder that each of us was not entirely alone.

Now and again we passed a small town, and since we were over Holland could imagine the peaceful folk still lying in their feather-beds, grunting as they turned on the other side. And all the time here were we roaring towards the front line.

There were sixty of us, but plenty of other aircraft were in the air near us—we only sighted them now as all the squadrons had climbed simultaneously so as not to offer an easy target to enemy flak. But even before we reached the forward positions, shells of all calibres started to explode among our ranks—we were flying into the gunfire of our own batteries which hadn't identified us. The effect was appalling. They were scoring hits with every salvo, since it was impossible to take avoiding action within our tight formation without colliding with a neighbour. Luck alone decided, and good luck had already deserted six out of my sixty comrades as we entered enemy territory.

Ten minutes more and we should reach our objective near Brussels. We were racing against the alarm report of our approach—down below the first observer posts must be scurrying to their telephones, commandants being hauled from their beds, flak personnel bustling to the guns, telephone girls interrupted in their reading, and finally the alarm bells ringing shrilly in the pilots' quarters at Brussels—Evère, the airfield on which our attack was directed. The smoke layer which lies above all great cities was hanging over Brussels, and as the other squadrons flew on towards their own objectives, we turned away to the east—and down on to Evère.

There lay the broad airfield with its familiar hangars right along our faintly glimmering sights. Hundreds of bombers and fighters were standing drawn-up on all sides of the field.

"Fire independently!"

Our bursts smacked into the parade. At that moment a few Spitfires were taking off—they moved right into the deadly hail, overturned, crashed or burst into flames. Bullets were ricochetting from the concrete runways and whizzing away again into the morning sky. The control-tower had often experienced our visits, but this time a quick-firing anti-aircraft gun was hammering from its roof. One of our men had already been lost. In a space of seconds I had traversed the field, and as I turned back I saw a pilot diving with desperate bravery against the gun on the control-tower. He and his enemy were firing simultaneously, their projectiles must surely have collided. I have never before seen such a mad, furious onslaught, the burst spraying among the guns' crews until none of either party were left alive.

The first fires were now blazing up among the parked aircraft. Among the soldiers running across the airfield for cover one fell prostrate as if dead, then jumped up again to run a little further—until he was hit and tumbled head over heels. Several mechanics were standing rooted to the spot by the walls of a hangar, and they too dropped, the guns spitting into every corner. As we continued our undisturbed diving on to the rows of bombers, heavy

163

blue-black clouds of smoke were rising from nearly forty aircraft.

Suddenly peacocks' eyes—British roundels—were racing towards us—Spitfires must have taken off from other airfields. It was hard now to distinguish friend from foe. Everyone scattered. Groups and flights curved in to attack the attackers and a wild chase began, a turmoil without front lines. Tracer flashed in all directions and damaged aircraft were diving earthwards with dark smoke clouds or blazing comet tails astern of them, huge umbrellas of smoke billowing up to the sky from where they struck. Several parachutes were dropping peacefully towards the earth.

I may well myself have been the only one who had not been embroiled in the fight.

Where was Werner? But as the thought ran through my head, I recognised his aircraft to my left—it was spinning in a vertical dive into the smoke-haze of the town.

"Werner! Werner!"

But he didn't answer any more. No, I had made no mistake, I could clearly make out his number, the great figure on his fuselage. For a moment things whirled before my eyes, and I flew on with difficulty ahead. It was my fault. I should have stayed near him!

Once more I called him up by radio. No reply! Dead! The same horrible feeling came over me that I had had when Ulrich crashed. The next moment I was being literally sick, retching where I sat.

I began steering automatically for home.

Far in front of me an old-fashioned English biplane was flying, doubtless doing the normal meteorological flight. I had no desire to shoot him down—and was in any case quite incapable of doing so—but I caught him up, throttled back and stationed myself a few paces to one side of him. The crew sat staring at me and at the German cross, their fear paralysing them. You're the people—I thought—you're the race of men who are murdering us, hunting the best of us down—and now Werner too! I waved them off with a contemptuous gesture, and they dived their old machine away towards the earth as if they had seen the devil himself.

Nevertheless, the sun's rays when it eventually rose reminded me that the life of the planet was still going on, and I came to my senses enough to bring my machine safe back home somehow and into its hangar.

"They're coming!" the mechanics were shouting. The noise of engines could be heard in the distance and we soon saw our armada heading towards the airfield in irregular formation. There seemed to be little more than thirty of them. Some swept low and shakily over the hangars and others with damaged undercarriages, slid along the ground to the whirling of high clouds of snow and came to rest with broken wings.

Vogel was walking beside me. His white shirt and white gloves were spattered with oil, and he was holding a handkerchief to his left eye.

"Werner has been killed," was all I said. I didn't give a thought to the possibility that he might only have been hurt.

"Oh, is that so?" he said, smiling wearily. "Is that so? . . ." he made a child-like, helpless gesture, his one eye giving me such a melancholy, serious look that I was startled.

"Meyer . . . crashed in flames . . . too."

Meyer II as well!

I discovered later that Meyer II had been shot down by the flak on the control-tower, and that it had been

Vogel who had annihilated the gun crews in his desperate attack. Only those who knew them both could understand that the one could not exist without the other. So it seemed inevitable that Vogel would have to die as well. Neither of them had ever talked of their parents, brothers or sisters, never gone on leave, written letters or even sought a girl's friendship—simply so as to be able to live undisturbed in their own world. Each had saved the life of the other many times. It was only in danger that they felt their best, as then they could make the greatest sacrifices for each other. Yet there was more in Vogel and Meyer II then the union of two airmen, and if both had succeeded in living through to peacetime, life perhaps might have altered their affection.

Nearly every one of our pilots had some particular experience to relate. But I was occupied with something different—as the hurried reports flew around the control-room, I began to work out the list of dead and missing. Maybe I was doing this because I didn't want to think, or because Werner was among the dead or for some other reason or for no reason at all. Still I was writing. The high-ups wanted to know how large the replacement would have to be. This unsentimental consideration was a perfectly sound one, for it was not the names but simply the numbers of the dead which reached the brain at the top with its calculating mechanism. This apparatus couldn't take the names into account, betokening as they did an incommunicable sorrow, the final loss of personalities, human beings whom wives and children, parents and friends mourned.

When I glanced up from my labours I saw only cheerful faces, blood-smeared or stiff with sweat as they might be—the faces of those who had won through. No—the dead were not with us. They were lying among glowing ashes, mutilated and charred, somewhere else. Someone mentioned a strange name to me.

"Who's that?"

"He stayed behind over Brussels. Quite a young chap," several of the fellows who had come here the day previously told me. So I knew the seventeen-year-old, too, had not returned.

Someone behind me leant forward over my shoulder and struck Werner's name from the list. I looked up.

"Not everyone who goes into a spin ends up in the happy hunting-grounds!" Werner told me, laughing. There outside stood his aircraft, its spars shot through and without its radio aerial.

CHAPTER XX

ALTHOUGH the end of the great war was approaching, the toll of victims increasingly continued. If Germany's fate was sealed, we had to fight on all the same to the last drop of blood. In the East, divisions were being bled white—in the West regiments collapsing, boys of fifteen and sixteen from the ranks of the Hitler Youth dying with the rest. The frontiers of the Reich had been broken and the Allies were pressing forward into it from all sides, the proof of American and English air power written now permanently in the sky.

Each time enemy aircraft were approaching we left the airfield, as there was no possibility of getting permission to take off, and we wanted to watch the spectacle from a safe distance. Vogel alone couldn't be stopped as soon as he saw an enemy. He flew with one eye only, his left one having been put out of action by a tiny shell-splinter, and now he wore a black shade over the dried-out sac where it had been. Although he attributed no less worth to his eyes than any other mortal, this loss didn't seem to be the cause of his continual brooding. No one who didn't know him could have believed it, but what grieved Vogel was that he still hadn't been killed. And as matters stood, he might have to wait a long time before being beaten in a fight. The Kommandeur had forbidden him to continue flying with one eye, but he ignored that—his orders to himself meant more to him: to fly, fight and fall.

In this spirit he would go up several times every day, nearly always return with victories to his credit and then sit brooding in his corner like an old man, over the tragedy of his solitary life: that he should always win and never be able to share his friend's fate.

One morning of sunny weather thirty Thunderbolts showed up, bombs hanging beneath their fuselages, and as we ran to our slit trenches only mad Vogel took off.

The fighter-bombers approached the centre of the airfield one by one and laid their "eggs" there. They must have had delayed-action fuses, as the charges didn't explode. The bombs, which weighed a hundredweight each, had not driven into the earth, moreover, but lay peacefully on the grassy surface. It was only half an hour later that we dared approach the dropping-point. There we had a pleasant surprise—the Thunderbolts had simply released their long-range tanks. We looked stupidly at one another but then began to laugh at the trick. Only gradually did we appreciate the chivalrous thought behind their action—they were warning us by this harmless token that real bombs would soon be following. Evidently the squadron-leader enjoyed such Klu-Klux-Klan mannerisms, and we thanked him for them.

"Vogel's dead!" somebody suddenly announced.

Guided by a mechanic to a plantation not far away, we there found the body of our dead comrade. His face was pressed into the ground, and as we raised his head the teeth began falling out of the open mouth. His body was pulped inside his flying-suit and his bones must have been smashed into hundreds of pieces by the impact. We were all the more upset precisely because we had every day expected this misfortune to happen.

Werner looked at the parachute release.

"Seems he couldn't pull it."

169

But every one of us knew that Vogel, hit and beaten in combat for the first time, had not wanted to open his parachute.

Werner bit his lip. "Lunacy!" he said, and I, too, shook my head uncomprehendingly, though we felt sympathy enough. As we stood by the corpse we looked at one another. The two of us here were all that were left of the Abbeville Boys. Which of us would be the next to go?

Towards midday large squadrons of Boeings approached. One wave after another passed over our airfield, and the bombs whistled down. As the muffled drumming and the line of high dust clouds extended towards us, we realized that we must pack our bags, that we should be leaving our beloved little town next morning, so as to await the next defeat, which might well be the last, elsewhere.

With April's alternate rain and sunshine, its storms and first spring flowers, German military strength was at its last gasp. The High Command was using drastic methods in its efforts to prevent the impending collapse of its troops. Generals met their end on the gallows. In the ruined towns old men and children were putting up road blocks of dustbins and petrol cans across bridges and roads—the unarmed *Volkssturm* was to bring the enemy to a halt.

Thousands of young, untrained girls had been recruited months previously for Luftwaffe units in the West, in order to take over the responsible work of experienced aircraft mechanics. Thousands of soldiers had left our formations as the Eastern Front badly needed bolstering up to stop the Russians. But they never got to the East. Instead they stayed for long periods in transit camps, and were finally transferred back to their old squadrons or squeezed into already overcrowded headquarters. Over on the enemy side, too, they knew how things looked here. While the Commander-in-Chief of the Luftwaffe was making an abusive address to the fighter personnel—we had to listen behind locked doors to gramophone records of his speech with its accusations of cowardice—the British radio was summoning us to desert.

Aircraft of all shapes and sizes and of types never before seen lay in hundreds round the edges of our airfield, and new machines were continually landing in the hope of finding shelter in this strange air parking-ground. Wounded from the Eastern Front, women auxiliaries from the north, weapons and even upholstery from all over the place were unloaded here. Commanders without troops, soldiers without their officers—were all assembling either in despair or in the unspoken hope that they would soon be able to go home. Only in one corner of the airfield was methodical activity still the order of the day, our camp, a restricted area which we shared with the turbine airmen. This was the test squadron to which George belonged.

The engineers who had indeed passed the pilots' examination, but who did not possess the flying experience and practice of the old hands, had a very difficult problem to solve. The mysterious failure of a new construction-series had remained unexplained: neither the calculations, the drawings nor the performance of the fast turbine single-seaters showed any defects. Yet no one dared take an aircraft into the air which even during take-off would not respond to the controls—nearly everyone who had sat in the cockpit of one of these aircraft had throttled right back again. Now they were building in new control-surfaces, replacing the transverse rudder and making additional adjustments to ensure success.

"I consider, *meine Herren*," the Chief Engineer declared, "that the solution of our problem could be of decisive importance."

We were standing with him at the take-off point where the experiment was about to take place. Three aircraft, racy-looking, twin-turbined single-seaters, were awaiting their test. A loudspeaker was connected to the radio link at the ground station to enable the pilot to inform those watching of his current situation and the experience gained.

The Chief Engineer himself climbed into the cockpit of the first aircraft. Its turbines howling wildly, driving the burning air astern with tremendous speed, the strange bird taxied a few metres forward.

The C.E. nodded at us from the cockpit. "I'm taking off," came through the loud-speaker. The howling of the turbines rose to an ear-piercing whine, increasingly painful to listen to and accompanied by an uncanny hollow undertone. The machine sped away, hurtling down the long runway.

"She wants to take off," the C.E. announced through the radio. "I'm bringing the stick back—back further— further still. Full power!"

He wasn't going to trim her. These were anxious moments. "Stick's right forward!" the pilot's excited voice came through again. "She's lifting—too steep!"

We could see she was putting her nose right up.

"I can't hold her any more. She's going over on her back!"

His voice rose to a yell on the last syllable. A sheet of flame flashed up and the smoke mushroom shot vertically into the sky. Seconds afterwards we heard the explosion.

"Well, it seems I must use trim," the young second engineer remarked, throwing away his cigarette. As he climbed into his machine his face was pale and he gave us a weary smile. We stepped back once again and covered our ears as he roared away.

"Wants to take off already, the brute!" he shouted. We knew well how feverishly he must be working in the cockpit. "I'm trimming nose-heavy," he continued calmly. "Still wants to put her nose up—more trim—I'm putting the stick forward. Now she's taking off! Good, still more trim. Good—flying well."

We could see her climbing with dark exhaust smoke just before the wood at the edge of the field.

"The trees are bloody close below me," the engineer called quickly. "The tops—too close—OUT!"

He was still shouting when the second conflagration broke high into the air. We stood below as if paralysed.

There was no way out of it—the defects could only be cured in flight up there in the air. Yet the engineers shook their heads.

"It isn't any good going on."

"Of course it is!" George said in a loud, sharp voice. "I'll fly. The take-off has just shown it can be done. But the runway was too short and the wood shouldn't be in the way."

"Stay down, George!" But he wouldn't hear a word from us.

"He's crazy," Werner whispered to me. "He'll crash just the same."

George had his aircraft pushed back as far as possible. The radio-van with the loud-speaker took us right up to the fence at the edge of the airfield.

"Empty half the tank," the cadet ordered. While they were doing so George joined us for a cigarette. He seemed to be quite sure of himself as he pointed to the engineers.

"Nearly all of them fly using their brains. You've got to fly by feel first, and only then can you bring your brains into play."

We still kept trying to turn him from his purpose, but "In a case like this, touch decides everything," he began again without listening, "and the feel for flying's a thing you've got to have in your backside. Some have got it and some haven't—I have!"

Since he had been wounded and suffered such severe concussion of the brain, George had been getting hold of some pretty strange ideas. We told one another he was crazy all right.

George took off. He was crouching right forward in the cockpit, and we held up our thumbs for him.

"Pressure forward and trimming," he reported— nothing more. The aircraft rose gradually from the ground and began climbing above the wood—higher— still higher.

"Bravo, George!"

Banking carefully, he turned back towards the airfield and then flew straight towards us. The machine made its approach very fast but silently, ran along the ground past us for a few hundred metres and took off again at a flat angle. Only then did a thin, muffled whine from the turbines reach our ears, and we asked him to land.

"No, I've got myself into the air. Now I want to find out what's wrong with the dragon."

He was evidently going to fly her to exhaustion! That couldn't succeed, since "fly to exhaustion" meant testing the machine's utmost capacity. And at such speeds it was scarcely possible to jump with a parachute.

The candidate for death had climbed in a few seconds to three thousand metres—then he put his nose down and dropped like a shooting-star out of the sky. A shout of triumph came through the loud-speaker.

"Just on a thousand!"

We held our breath, then yelled, "Pull out, you idiot!"

Gradually, very gradually, her nose drew up once more until he was once again in the normal flying position—he must have had to haul the stick back with the force of both his arms. Now he climbed obliquely away into the sky, trailing streams of white condensation. A few moments later a sharp metallic report whipped through the air.

"Rivets drawn," he was gasping, still breathless from the effort of the dive and pull-out, "a whole row of rivets and plates from the trailing-edges of the wings have been torn away."

The engineers looked at one another joyfully—so *that* was what was wrong—and gratefully above them to where George had gradually brought his aircraft horizontal. We hoped he would throttle back and jump, but he didn't want to abandon the machine, as only the freshly caused damage could give evidence of the defect they had sought so long.

So George came in to land. "I hope I can hold her off," he called hoarsely, and as she flew in low towards the airfield we were watching pretty anxiously.

"Four hundred, three-eighty, three-fifty—three-twenty —two-seventy—she's getting flabby."

For a moment we thought we could see him floating unstably, then the finely drawn silhouette of the machine rose clear again above the horizon.

"Drops too fast, opened my throttle—she was going to drop her nose even at two-fifty—the bloody cow!"

After that George became silent. He had to concentrate on a difficult landing—he would have to touch down at 250 kilometres an hour!

The aircraft whistled like an arrow above our heads, only two or three metres up. Now came the most difficult moment, and perhaps the most dangerous, of the whole flight: the needle of the air-speed indicator had to show 250 kilometres—no more and no less, as the wheels touched the ground. At least a thousand eyes were straining to see the outcome of this desperate venture.

Now! The left wing was on the point of dropping as the undercarriage struck the ground.

George was sitting on the grass only a few feet from the fence at the other side of the aerodrome when we arrived to congratulate him.

"Every landing's a crash landing," he remarked, smiling, "if only from a height of fifty, thirty or twenty centimetres."

That evening, as George, Werner and I were sitting together, Werner was talking enthusiastically about the new turbine-fighter.

"Five hundred of *them*, and Goering wouldn't need to be called a fraud any longer."

George shook his head.

"Well, I have seen almost as many along the *Autobahns* in South Germany—though they weren't operational. But where are you going to find room in them for your guns? Besides, they break up in the air and can scarcely get off the ground. Hopeless! And apart from that, it's all nonsense, anyway, isn't it? I just don't want any more weapons."

At this observation Werner gave us quite a shock by

the black, mistrustful look he gave first one and then the
other of us. George replied with nothing but an ironical
look, but seeing Werner was taking the thing seriously he
leant over towards him.

"Now listen, old chap, you really aren't the man in the
moon. You can see quite well from day to day which way
the cat is jumping—you can't really mean to tell me that
we can still win the war."

"Yes, I know none of you believe it any longer,"
Werner came back angrily. "But I'm telling you perhaps
we shall win the war quicker than you imagine possible.
'Five minutes past twelve' is what the Führer said, don't
you remember? He doesn't let us fight on to no purpose."

"Ah," George began to jeer, "you're still dreaming of
a Father Christmas with dear little V-weapons, nice little
atom-bombs and so on!"

Werner walked tensely to the window, doubtless to
hide his inward emotion.

"Out there they're running away in their millions," he
murmured, more to himself than to us, "weak-mindedly,
with their hearts in their boots, just running away from it.
The heroes have become shirkers and the idealists—
traitors! Most of them have forgotten the great idea—
but I'll tell you one thing——" he turned to us, "if that
idea is destroyed it'll drag everything with it over the
precipice, our country and our people. The Führer's idea
will be prostituted and his Reich turned into a gigantic
slave-market."

George filled up the glasses. "You're a good chap,
Werner, but don't talk so big. Come and take the weight
off and have some brandy! Prost! To the shirkers!"
George raised his glass. Putting it down, "You wanted
to catch me out over that business of no one wanting to
fight and all that," he went on. "But I've got my own

idea, too, and quite a good one—new, what's more. I'd like to explain it to you, and perhaps then you'll understand me."

Slightly embarrassed, and probably for this reason rather pompously, he drew out a small illustrated booklet and threw it down in front of him. On the title page, in large red letters was written, *The Battle of Britain— August–October*, 1940, *published by the Air Ministry in London*.

"Where did you get that? It's enemy propaganda!"

"But it's good! Where did I get it from? My last opponent—the last I shall ever have beaten in my life— sent me this as a memento. Look at this!" George turned the first page and showed us a large picture.

Nine young Royal Air Force pilots were walking laughing and talking in a line towards the camera. They might have just turned from looking at one of their Spit- fires which was standing behind them with wings spread wide.

"Have a good look at those faces!" George suggested. "They might just as well belong to us."

And in fact the features of certain of the pilots were distinctly reminiscent of some of our own comrades'.

"Now you see what I'm getting at," said George.

CHAPTER XXI

WERNER was standing silently beside me beneath the stars of a May night. Hitler had shot himself. Werner was only one among millions whose hopes had been carried with him to the grave. He was unable to grasp it all yet, for he had known nothing except a deep, firm belief in the idol which had now been smashed. The Germany for which Werner had fought in good faith had died with Hitler.

"I haven't learnt anything except how to believe in him," he said tonelessly. "Now I've gone flabby, I haven't any purpose any more."

The great mass of stars stretched limitlessly above the two small human creatures that were us. How vast the extent of human suffering is, I thought—how much pain there must be stored up in this universe.

The clock of the small north German town was striking midnight. I put out my hand to shake Werner's—to-day was his twentieth birthday. And at that we separated, without saying another word.

I was just going to bed when Hinterschallers came in.

"There's a girl downstairs—guess who?"

"I'm off to bed."

"Danielle, man, Danielle!"

Hinterschallers pushed her into my room. She looked at me for a long while.

"I'm so glad you've paid us a visit!"

"I don't want to pay a *visit*," she replied. For a moment I tried to understand what she was trying to say. Then I understood—she was going to stay.

"I could go back to France soon, but I don't want to any more."

"But it will be very hard, my dear. Germany will be forced to surrender in a few days' time. Germany has been beaten."

"You have said that once before. But that isn't the point."

"Well, what do you hope to do?"

"Nothing. Nothing except to be able to stay here near the aeroplane which Ulrich used to fly and the uniform he wore, and the men with whom he shared all his experiences and who are like him. I want to have him near me again to close my eyes and hear the engine of his machine —to half close them and see him walking across from the hangar. I want to stay near to where he is."

"It would be better for you to forget rather than to have such fancies. In a few days time we won't be flying or even wearing uniform any more."

Looking at the ground, she spoke gently.

"Then I shall start looking for the man who is like Ulrich."

"But he can't *be* Ulrich."

"Why shouldn't he be the Ulrich I mean! I can count the hours I spent with Ulrich on my ten fingers. I loved him much more than I knew about him. What little I knew, too, doesn't bind me to him. But I shall keep looking for the rest of him, to hold onto always."

"So you want to find someone who's like him, his double, more or less?"

"Yes, I'm looking for his double, but the double of what he was, a double who has his heart."

"And do you think you have found him?"

"Yes, it is quite possible I have found him."

She gave me her hand, and turned away.

With the first rays of the sun we drove out to the airfield. Danielle, for whom Hinterschallers had some-how got hold of a room, had already got up to come with us.

Troop-transports were landing in a continuous stream, women and children spilling out of their great hulls. Some might prefer to sleep on, but our only desire was to get the latest from the front. Perhaps the war was already over!

Before the hangar the chief mechanic was standing, with the fitter who had so often foretold the fate of airmen I had known.

"Any news?"

"These people are from Stettin," the chief mechanic told us, indicating the transports. "They're evacuating the women and children, as the place is surrounded by the Russians. They say that Spitfires are continually diving on the transports from a great height above the town and shooting them down."

Werner and I looked at one another—the same thought had occurred to both of us. Should we take off? Perhaps we would be able to save a transport or two from destruc-tion. But to-day was Werner's birthday, and it had always been the custom not to send birthday-boys into the air. Werner was hesitating—it was the first time I had ever seen him uncertain of himself. I knew quite well what was going on in his mind: he was afraid to go into action without the great objective and the strength of his beliefs. Germany was dead for him, and he couldn't imagine any other.

Still, he had seen the expressions of the refugee women and children.

"We're taking off," he said. "Get our aircraft ready!"

As he walked across with the chief mechanic to our machines, the fitter held me back.

"Don't fly to-day!" he said earnestly. "I didn't want to say anything more to anyone, but the war'll be over in a few days, and you don't have to get killed. I'm telling you, don't fly to-day! You'll never come back!"

Then, before I had recovered from my fright, he moved off. A nauseating pang shot through me. I didn't want to die, and now especially! For a long time now I had glimpsed a new and lovely purpose in life behind the ruins of the present. Months ago it had only been a thought to flirt with, but now it was a clear, fresh aim, one to live for. The way to it might well take me through thorns and swamps, shame and hunger, but I already felt inside me the strength and the love which could open up the road. It was worth while now to live for the Germany which was lying prostrate, drained of its lifeblood—and which needed the strength of free, courageous hearts for its recovery. And I was thinking of Danielle. . . .

The roar of the engines jerked me from my thoughts. Werner was already sitting in his aircraft. I ran across to him—he must be told what the fitter had said. But as I stood on the wing beside him I felt ashamed to be shouting it out to him.

"The fitter?" he called. But he seemed to have guessed what I wanted to say, and switched off his engine.

"Yes, he said so."

Werner spoke softly.

"I won't come back. I can feel it. Why should I? Everything's pointless now, everything's gone!"

His arm was hanging limply over the side of the cockpit. Danielle had come across to us. Werner was staring at the instrument panel, and I looked at the girl. No one said a word. But Danielle and I were certainly thinking the same: there's good and there's evil, both lying between what is right and what is wrong. . . . Like Ulrich, I wanted to keep to that. And as I had made my decision I knew that Danielle had hoped for this.

Probably from awkwardness, the mechanic had started to talk again.

"Yes, my mother lives in Stettin. But I haven't seen her here yet. She's bound to be there still."

"I'm taking off," we replied in the same breath. As I climbed in, Danielle stretched out her hand. She was crying, but her voice was happy.

"Ulrich's back again now. I'll be waiting for you."

Once more our aircraft thundered across the field, rose laboriously from the ground and climbed steeply upwards. As we roared low across the airfield and the hangars I saw Danielle once again. She was waving—had soon become a tiny dot in the distance—a pair of large, dark eyes gazing after me. . . .

The bright rising ball of the sun stood out clear and rayless beneath a steel-blue sky. The small needle of the altimeter crept steadily round its arc from figure to figure: eight thousand metres, the safest height at which to approach Stettin unmolested.

On the right and behind us must lie Hamburg with its docks and harbours beneath a blue-black pall, and far astern on the horizon Heligoland. Between the deep blue of the North Sea and the Baltic lay the last stretches of north German soil which the enemy armies were not yet marching over. Visibility could not have been better, though the horizon hung suspended in a thin leaden haze. The earth's curvature could clearly be made out, the solemn rolling of the gigantic ball almost perceptible. Our exalted view of such immensity of space gave me an added breadth of spirit and a strange feeling of intimacy with the maker of it all.

I had completely forgotten my fears. But all the same it was a very dangerous thing to dream dreams up here in this neighbourhood. I had better not enjoy my view across the world too much, for all around me murder was lurking. Any moment might decree I must either kill or be killed. So once more I made an effort to keep my eyes intently directed astern and above me into the ether.

Suddenly there they were, the British, lying in wait to pounce on our vulnerable backs.

I counted twenty fighters, most likely Spitfires, which we hadn't expected at this altitude. They appeared to be following us and were a thousand metres above. Twenty short white condensation trails and twenty pairs of roundels menaced us wickedly. I felt my fear once more— the fitter's pronouncement was coming true. Never before in the air had I felt the possibility of death so strongly as now. It made me shiver as though I were frozen. A string seemed drawn tight around my neck, a great lump sat in my throat.

I still hoped that the Tommies might not have seen us. But here they came, diving down on us!

"Werner, they're coming!"

There was no point in diving away. I estimated the British were still a thousand metres behind me—the dance would begin in a few seconds. I'm already looking down the gun-barrels of an enemy hanging huge and close behind me. I immediately follow my instinct and slip my aircraft sideways.

The enemy's burst is like a glowing string of pearls

from his gun—which whisper past me to the left. It's blinding. I bring my aircraft slightly lower and the death-dealing tracer flies a fraction of a second late over my head. At last I'm able to pull round into a counter-attack. The sun swings round too until it's at my back, and my thoughts fly ahead: now for the dog-fight! But at the same instant peacocks' eyes come swarming all about me, countless trails of smoke and tracer criss-crossing the hornet-swarm. Each sting can be mortal, and we're flying for our lives between them.

For a few seconds I'm free to look round. Werner, I can see, is hanging alone and helpless in the middle of a swarm of Englishmen, like a German grenadier finding himself fallen-in on an English parade. The Tommies astern of him daren't fire for fear of hitting the English-man ahead of him; and neither can Werner shoot the man in front, as he would himself receive a mortal burst from the fellow behind him the instant he had done so. I'm working out in the few seconds I have how I can aid Werner, whom I can hear in my earphones desperately calling for help. The Englishman ahead of him is already trying to clear the line of fire.

I can feel exactly what lies before me if I dive into that mass which will be spitting death a hundred times over. I know I shall be throwing myself to the dogs by doing so—but, then, I had already thought of that.

I turn steeply into the swarm of my enemies, and run into a hail of glowing shot and bursting shell. For an instant, I think I'm going to be rammed. But in a second or two I reach Werner. I fly in from the side at him and have actually to train my sights on him to hit the English-man who is just on his tail.

My guns crash out and the whole aircraft is shaken by the recoil—but in the same instant Werner dives away

185

on fire, as his attacker draws past my sights—until he too spins down in flames.

"Get out, Werner!" I called. "Jump!"

"I can't," he shouts, "I just can't. . . ."

At this instant I get a stunning shock as though everything has been smashed. My aircraft has been hit and dives away vertically downwards. I fling up my left arm instinctively before my eyes and my right hand feels for the handle to release the cockpit hood. I press it sharply down, twice, three times . . . there's an uncanny muffled roar and flames burst through the bulkhead in front of me! Rubber, oil, phosphorus and petrol are burning, biting into my nose and eyes.

I'm still sitting paralysed on my narrow seat, which serves also as a container for five hundred devilish litres of petrol. I'm nerveless and irresolute, with all the time one thought and one thought only running through my mind: well, this is what always had to come.

But second thoughts produce a more conscious reaction. I tear myself free of my harness and try to jump. But I can't get my left leg free, it's got jammed. I can't jump, so I'm going to be burnt alive! And only now does my real situation come home to me. I cry out in my despair and pain—the one time I do so. Then I turn away to one side and huddle myself down. I'm shivering before what I know is coming, in fact the thought of it almost submerges the hellish pain of the burning.

Meanwhile the aircraft is hurtling towards the ground. Through all my imaginings I know I'm getting closer to it at two hundred metres every second. The roaring flames are eating their way closer and closer to my body. My left arm is protecting my face, but I've the impression my jammed leg must already be charred to ashes. I await the end with fear and curiosity. Now the impact's coming

—now—now. My brain is strained to bursting-point, and I can feel Friend Hein's cold arms about me. So this is it.

"Now I have been killed. I have done my duty."

I say this loudly and firmly, and the words give me a kind of peace and confidence. I think of Danielle and then of myself. A gleam of hope leaps in me like a blazing spark.

Once more I struggle with all my power to escape. I will—I must go on living! Danielle is a goal for my life! I'm astonished by the superhuman energy I'm now capable of, in my struggles to free my jammed leg. My knee is being twisted, and the left side of my pelvis seems to be slowly breaking. But at last the leg comes free.

Still, in all I do, the torturing question's still there. When is the crash coming—the explosion? Can I still make it? With the whole strength of my arms and legs I force myself out of my seat. It can only be done slowly, with a desperate use of will-power. I'm still pinned against the body of the aircraft and don't know how to get clear of it—and among these flames I can't open my eyes. I'm thinking I can't hold death at bay any longer.

And then all at once the giant grip of the airflow tears me free.

I'm falling—clear, released from the burning monster! The searing heat and the pain have faded away, their place taken by a feeling of blessed happiness. For a moment I see the ground, the shape of a tree—dreadfully large. Only seconds are left before I shall meet the earth! I regain control of myself enough to reach for the parachute release handle. It isn't there—my hand's pulled up by the rush of air.

My senses are reeling. But I *will* live. I *will*. . . . Trembling, I've somehow got the handle and pull it with my last strength. The parachute bursts upwards with a hollow report. With the jerk the harness cuts deep into my thighs.

It's peacefully quiet, and I'm floating. I can't yet take it in, still can't believe it. But as I look up the white silk of the parachute is billowing above me against the bright blue sky, here and there a little torn.

Some seconds later I hit the earth heavily in a field. I pull off my harness and rise laboriously to my feet. The smell of burning phosphorus is still stinging my nose, and there's a roasted meat smell. When I look down at myself my flying suit's hanging on me in charred rags, my arms and legs are half-raw, half-burnt bloody flesh, with smeared strips of skin hanging from the edges, and the fat trickling down.

Whatever can my face be looking like? Mildly curious as I am, it's a pity I haven't a mirror handy. I haven't any pain either. I know just one thing: notwithstanding greatest danger only lasted thirty seconds, I have grown years older.

With an effort I call out "Hallo!" to the farmer standing over there, and my voice sounds thin and weak like a man calling for help in his sleep. It's funny it's so feeble. The farmer seems to have heard all right, though, he's running towards me. Yes, he's from this world all right, it's I who have come from another.

The bells are beginning to ring out above the roofs of villages and towns. It seems at first they were wanting to give my dead friend a last peal. But I realize that instead they are announcing peace, and a new life.

When the guns of the Second World War at last fell silent, Germany's airmen shared the fate of every soldier. They waited behind the barbed-wire of prison camps on their own or on foreign soil, or wandered about looking for a new reason to live. Many of them were turned away at the gates of universities or at the doors of shops, offices and factories. What had airmen learnt to do?

So they looked back again into the clouds—their natural surroundings. But only a few, in foreign countries, were able to get back to them, those uniform spaces which know no signposts.

So still, when an aircraft streaks across the sky or birds of passage battle beneath dirty, grey clouds against autumn storms, the broken-winged German airmen pause below. They have a yearning to return to the clouds, an ache for the sky.